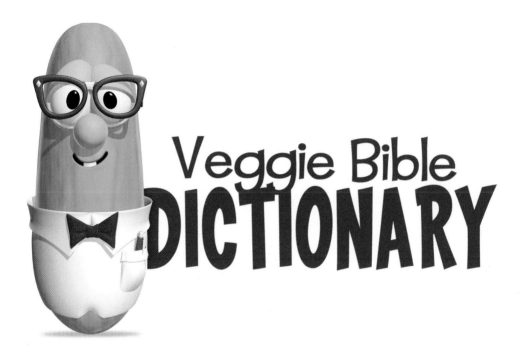

Veggie Bible
DICTIONARY

VeggieTales®
VeggieConnections™
Connecting to a Powerful Relationship with God.

Veggie Bible
DICTIONARY

by Cindy Kenney and Karen Brothers

BIG IDEA

INTEGRITY®
PUBLISHERS
family

www.bigidea.com

www.integritypublishing.com

VeggieConnections Bible Dictionary
ISBN: 1-59145-252-X
Copyright © 2005 by Big Idea, Inc.
Illustrations copyright © 2005 by Big Idea, Inc.

Requests for information should be addressed to:
Integrity Publishing, 5250 Virginia Way, Suite 110, Brentwood, TN 37027

———————————————

Written by: Cindy Kenney and Karen Brothers
Contributing Writer: Karl Pradel
Editors: Cindy Kenney
Art Direction: John Trent
Layout & Design: Jim Stelluto

Kenney, Cindy, 1959-
VeggieConnections Bible dictionary / by Cindy Kenney, Karl Pradel, and Karen Brothers. p. cm.
Summary: "Dictionary is filled with definitions that will help children understand words from the Bible
and words having to do with Veggie World characters"--Provided by publisher.
  ISBN 1-59145-252-X (hardcover)
  1. Bible--Dictionaries, Juvenile. I. Pradel, Karl. II. Brothers, Karen. III. Title.
  BS440.K35 2005
  220.3--dc22
  2004027044

Why A *Veggie Bible Dictionary*?

VeggieTales® is dedicated to bringing biblical messages to children and families everywhere. That's how we connect with you, by helping to bridge a connection between you and the most important words ever written. So it seemed a natural next step for us to provide both churches and families alike with a Bible Dictionary that will help kids learn about the words they read and hear about in the Bible.

Next, we decided to toss in some fun! To help you learn more about your favorite characters from VeggieTales and some of those wacky words in the stories they make, we tossed in some of those words too. Then we topped off some definitions with some special commentary from your friends, Bob the Tomato and Larry the Cucumber.

The *Veggie Bible Dictionary* works as a great tool with the VeggieConnections™ curriculum program. Children can be guided to the dictionary to look up words they will find in every lesson. The dictionary also works as a wonderful resource for a Sunday school or midweek teacher of any curriculum, and as a terrific book for the entire family.

When kids open their *Veggie Bible Dictionary* we hope that it will be both an educational event and bring a smile to their face. Kids will want to open their Bible dictionary because they want to hear more about what their favorite characters from VeggieTales® have to say! And guess what? They'll be learning God's Word in the process!

How Should You Use Your *Veggie Bible Dictionary?*

A dictionary is a useful connection tool. It helps to better connect you to God's Word by helping you learn what it means. It helps you to learn how to better say that word, too. In the *Veggie Bible Dictionary*, we help to connect you to more words that bring the Bible words into your everyday life. When you combine these words, it will connect you with a lifetime guide that will help you discover a relationship with God that can last forever!

So where do you begin?

1. If there is a Bible word, a lesson word, or a VeggieTales word that you want to know more about, look it up.
2. The dictionary is in alphabetical order. That means it starts at A and ends with Z. Look under the correct letter to begin to find the word you are looking for.
3. You will find Heading Words at the top left-hand and top right-hand corner of each page. The top left-hand word is the first word on that page, and the top right-hand word is the very last one on that page. Everything else in between are the words that are alphabetically located between them.
4. Some of the Bible word definitions will tell you where in the Bible you can find it. Some of the VeggieTales words will tell you one of the videos you can find it!
5. And now the best part! Don't forget that some of the silly comments are from Bob and Larry. These comments are in colored type because they are . . . well, silly! Always remember Bob and Larry want you to have fun!

Aaron (AIR-uhn) A Levite and elder brother of Moses who helped lead the Hebrews out of Egypt.

abandon (uh-BAN-dun) To leave behind or give up on. God will never abandon us. See *Deuteronomy 4:31.* Don't abandon your vegetables, because they are quite good for you.

Abba, father (AB-uh) Another name for God. Early Christians used this word in speaking to God.

Abednego (a-BED-nih-go) Daniel's friend who was protected in the fiery furnace with two others. The Veggie-Tales video "Rack, Shack, and Benny" was based on Abednego & his friends Shadrach and Meshach.

Abel (AY-bul) The second son of Adam and Eve who was killed by his brother, Cain.

Abigail (AB-ih-gale) Wife of King David.

ability (uh-BILL-ih-tee) A skill. Jesus told a parable about talents and abilities in *Matthew 25:15.* Jimmy and Jerry have an uncanny ability to eat anything in sight.

ABOARD the pirate's ship.

aboard (uh-BORD) On board a ship, train, aircraft, or other passenger vehicle. Seymour Schwenk invited Cavis and Milward aboard his rocket-car in "The Star of Christmas."

A

Abraham (AY-brah-ham) The first of the Old Testament patriarchs, husband of Sarah, and the father of Isaac.

Absalom (AB-sah-lum) One of King David's sons who tried to take over David's kingdom.

abundance (uh-BUN-dens) A lot of something. Before learning about thankfulness, Madame Blueberry had an abundance of, well . . . everything.

abyss (uh-BISS) A gulf so deep or a space so great that it cannot be measured. The gourds flew into space and were frightened by the black abyss that surrounded them—until they landed on a planet and found some new friends!

accept (ak-SEPT) To receive (something offered), especially with gladness or approval. See how Jesus wants us to accept one another in *Romans 15:7.*

accomplish (uh-KOM-plish) To succeed in doing; to finish or complete something. The Pirates Who Don't Do Anything regularly accomplish a whole lot of nothing.

account (uh-KOUNT) To keep track of; to provide an explanation for; a story. Larry has a hard time accounting for the whereabouts of his hairbrush.

ACQUIRE Larry's hairbrush.

acquire (uh-KWYR) To get something. Larry would really like to acquire some hair to go along with his hairbrush. "Oh Where Is My Hairbrush?"

Acts (AKTS) The fifth book of the New Testament written by Luke; focuses on the Holy Spirit.

Adam (AD-um) The first man and husband of Eve.

adopt (uh-DOPT) To take by choice into a relationship; to accept or take on.

adorn (A-dorn) to improve the appearance by adding something that is not essential.

afraid (uh-FRAYD) Scared or frightened. See *Psalm 56:3* for what to do when you feel afraid. Junior was afraid of Frankencelery. "Where's God When I'm S-scared?"

agape (uh-GAH-pay) Being in a state of wonder; abundance of love.

agreement (uh-GREE-ment) A promise between two people or groups of people; or between a person or group of people and God.

Ahab (A-hab) A king of Israel who did not believe in God and worshiped the false god, Baal.

A

aid (AID) To help or assist. To offer support or encouragement. Junior offered aid to his neighbor, even though his neighbor was from out of town.

Junior's **AFRAID**.

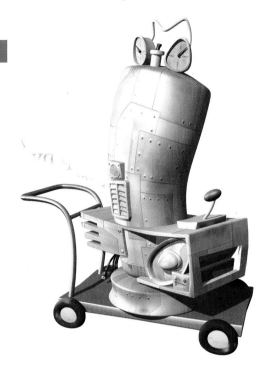

AIR COMPRESSOR

air compressor (AIR kom-PRESS-er) A device used to force air into inflatable objects. It is highly unusual to frost a cake with an air compressor.

aisle (I-ull) A walkway in between pews/benches in a place of worship.

alabaster (AL-u-bast-er)A smooth, usually white, and nearly see-through stone. In Bible times, perfume and oil were kept in alabaster jars.

almighty (all-MITE-ee) Having unlimited power. God is often called, "Almighty" in the Bible.

alone (uh-LOHN) To be all by yourself; without help. Daniel was not alone in the lions' den.

alpha (AL-fuh) The first one; the beginning. See *Revelation 1:8.*

altar (ALL-ter) A raised place where religious rites or sacrifices are made.

amazing (uh-MAY-zing) An expression used when something is really wonderful. Isn't it amazing that a zucchini can run a chocolate factory?

ambition (am-BIH-shun) An eager or strong desire to achieve something; a goal; an objective; a dream. "Do nothing out of selfish ambition or vain conceit . . . " See *Philippians 2:3.* It is Lyle's ambition to be an honest and kindly Viking.

amen (ah-MEN or AY-men) An expression used at the end of prayers meaning it is so.

Bob is Larry's **AMIGO.**

amigo (uh-MEE-go) The word for friend in Spanish often used by Larry the Cucumber. Bob is Larry's main amigo!

Amos (AY-mus) The thirtieth book of the Old Testament; named after a shepherd who speaks strongly about the poor and God's love for them.

Ananias (an-ih-NY-us) The man in Damascus who, in a vision, was commanded to go and heal Saul's blindness.

anchor (ANG-cur) A heavy object attached to a ship by a cable or rope and cast overboard to keep the ship in place. The Pirates Who Don't Do Anything rarely used their anchor because it would have required them to do something.

ancient (AIN-chent) Very, very old.

Andrew (AN-drew) One of Jesus' twelve disciples. See *Mark 1:16–18*.

angel (AIN-jel) A spiritual messenger from God.

angry (ANG-ree) A reaction or a feeling to something that really upsets you; usually negative. James gives us advice about anger in *James 1:19*. Larryboy once had a nasty encounter with some angry eyebrows.

Annas (AN-us) One of the high priests in Jerusalem when Jesus was alive.

ANNIE

Annie (AN-nee) A young teenaged Veggie character Annie is a scallion and is George's granddaughter.

announcement (uh-NOUNS-ment) A message that is made known to an audience. An announcement was made to the crew of the U.S.S. Applepies that the popcorn meteor was no longer a threat thanks to Jimmy and Jerry.

anoint (uh-NOINT) To put oil on.

answer (AN-ser) To give a reply to a question.

Antioch (AN-tee-ahk) A city of southern Turkey on the Orontes River near the Mediterranean Sea; an early center of Christianity.

anxious (ANK-shus) To be worried about something. See how Paul tells us not to be anxious. See *Philippians 4:6*.

apostle (uh-PAH-sul) Someone special who preaches the gospel; one of Jesus' twelve disciples and Paul. *Mark 3:14*.

appearance (uh-PEER-ens) The way you look. You would greatly affect your appearance if you were to put peanut butter in your hair.

APPLY
the brakes.

apply (uh-PLIE) To put into action. Despite applying the brakes, Bob the Tomato was unable to control the van.

appreciate (uh-PREE-shee-ate) To be grateful for; to be thankful, or show thankfulness; to understand something that has been done. Archibald doesn't appreciate Larry's silly songs.

Aquila (AK-wi-la) A Jewish Christian from Rome who traveled with Paul. He and his wife, Priscilla, worked as tentmakers. Read *Acts 18* to read about Aquila and Priscilla.

archangel (ark-AIN-jel) The leader of God's angels. His name was Michael. Read in *1 Thessalonians 4:16* how the archangel will appear when Christ returns.

Archibald Asparagus (AR-chee-bald uh-SPAIR-uh-gus) This Veggie has an English accent and often plays the part of leaders, such as King Darius, the Mayor of Flibber- o-loo, and of course Alfred, Larryboy's butler.

ARCHIBALD ASPARAGUS

A

A

ark (ARK) A large boat that God requested Noah to build. See *Genesis 6:14* An ark is a cool place to skateboard.

ark of the covenant The special box which held the Ten Commandments.

ARMCHAIR

armchair (ARM-chair) A comfy chair with side structures to support the arms or elbows; a great place to read your Bible or think about relationships with God.

armor (AR-mr) Items to put on your body to protect it from being hurt. Christ-ians are told to put on the full armor of God. See *Ephesians 6:10-18.*

army (AR-mee) A group of trained soldiers; a large crowd ready to do something.

arrest (uh-REST) To be captured by authorities. Charles Pincher was under arrest for stealing.

ascend (uh-SEND) To go up. Jesus ascended into heaven after he was crucified. See *Acts 1:9.*

ash (ASH) Fine debris left after a fire.

Asher (ASH-er) Joseph's brother, son of Jacob.

Asia (AY-zhuh) A province during Bible times.

assemble (uh-SEM-bull) To gather together.

assure (uh-SHOOR) To give words of comfort or confidence to; to provide a guarantee for something. Bob assured Larry that he was a very good friend.

astonish (uh-STON-ish) To fill with sudden wonder or amazement. Would it astonish you if I were to fill Larryboy's boots with liverwurst?

atonement (ah-TONE-ment) Making amends and asking someone to forgive you after you have done something wrong. See how a High Priest had to make atonement in *Hebrews 2:17*.

attention (uh-TEN-shun) A close or careful observing; to listen, concentrate, or notice.

attitude (AT-tih-tood) The way you think and feel about something. With a positive attitude there is very little Bob cannot accomplish.

authority (aw-THOR-uh-tee) Someone who is in charge; permission to do something. Sheriff Bob has the authority to arrest criminals in Dodgeball City.

Italian Scallion **AWAITS** the opening.

await (uh-WAYT) To wait for. The Italian Scallion had to await the opening of Gourd's Gym. Don't confuse that with lifting weights at Gourd's Gym!

awesome (AW-sum) Something that is super great and double-fantastic; something overwhelming and wonderful. See how God is awesome in *Psalm 47:2*.

Awful Alvin (AW-fewl AL-vin) A supervillain that loved to dance with his lamp named "Lampy."

Baal (BAY-ul) The Babylonian name of a false god whom the Egyptians worshiped.

baby (BAY-bee) A young infant or toddler. The baby Jesus lay in the manger.

Baby Lou (BAY-bee LOO) Laura carrot's younger brother.

backpack (BAK-pak) A cloth storage bag that you can wear on your back.

bad (BAD) Naughty.

badge (BADJ) A shiny metal pin. Sheriff Bob and Little Joe wear badges to identify themselves in Dodgeball City.

bald monkey (BALD MUNG-kee) A monkey with no hair: "Like butter on a bald monkey."

ballad (BAL-led) A narrative poem, intended to be sung. A ballad is not something to try and sing with a mouthful of candycorn. "The Ballad of Little Joe."

bamboo (bam-BOO) A type of wood that resembles a hollow tube. In "Larry's Lagoon," the professor discovers how many contraptions can be built out of bamboo and coconuts.

bandit (BAN-dit) A bad guy. The Milk Money Bandit was one of Bumblyburg's most notorious thieves.

banquet (BANG-kwit) A big party with lots and lots of yummy food.

baptize (BAP-tize) To christen and cleanse a person spiritually. John the Baptist prepared for the baptism of Jesus. See *Matthew 3:11.*

Barabbas (bah-RAB-us) The robber and murderer who was set free instead of Jesus when Pilate offered to release one of the two prisoners.

BARBARA MANATEE

Barbara Manatee (BAR-bar-a MAN-a-tee) Larry's much loved stuffed animal. "Barbara Manatee, you are my mon ami."

Barnabas (BAR-nah-bus) A Christian who was known for being kind and encouraging to others.

Bartholomew (bar-THOL-o-mew) One of the 12 disciples that followed Jesus.

Bathsheba (bath-SHE-buh) Wife of King David and mother of Solomon.

battle (BA-tul) To fight; an encounter between opposing forces. "Some kings love horses and some kings love cattle, some kings love leading their troops into battle."

bay (BAY) A cove or inlet of water. A bay is a great place to find vacationing scampi.

beach (BEECH) A sandy area in front of a body of water. A beach is not a good place to test out a new vacuum.

beady eyes (BEE-dee IZE) Small, round eyes that are up to no good. Given the choice between having small, shifty, beady eyes or no eyes at all, Mr. Lunt chose no eyes.

beam (BEEM) To radiate light; shine.

Madame Blueberry thinks her hair looks like a **BEAST.**

beast (BEEST) An evil creature. Madame Blueberry thinks her hair looks like a beast on a windy day.

beaten (BEE-ten) To get hit or banged up. The good Samaritan helped a man who was beaten by robbers.

beatitude (bee-AT-tih-tood) A term used for the teach-ings of Jesus about how to act in our lives. See *Matthew 5:3–12.*

Beelzebub (bee-EL-ze-bub) Also named Baal-Zebub, this was a false god of the Philistines.

beg (BEG) An intense request; to deeply feel the need for something. Jonah begged the Pirates to take him to Tarshish.

beginning (be-GIN-ning) a starting point; the start of Creation. See *Genesis 1:1.*

behalf (be-HAFF) To do something in the interest of someone else. On behalf of Palmy the palm tree (at the Veggie Lagoon), please stop eating so many coconuts.

believe (be-LEEV) To have faith in. Paul talks about believing in Jesus in *Romans 3:22.*

believer (be-LEE-ver) Someone who has trust in God and knows God to be true.

belly (BELL-ee) Another word for tummy. When Jonah disobeyed God, he ended up in the belly of a whale.

belly button (BELL-ee BUH-tun) The thing on your tummy that either sticks in or out. "The Belly Button Song" is a favorite VeggieTales silly song.

belong (be-LONG) To fit in. Larry is so glad his lips belong to him.

benefit (BEN-e-fit) Something that offers something good to a person or thing; a useful aid or help. It really benefits Larry if Bob helps him prepare for a benefit that will help kids who are sick.

Benjamin (BEN-juh-min) Joseph's youngest brother.

Benny (BEN-nee) A Veggie character played by Larry the Cucumber in "Rack, Shack, and Benny" representing the young man Abednego, who emerged unharmed from the fiery furnace of Babylon.

beret (buh-RAY) A round, soft, brimless cap that fits snugly and is often worn angled to one side. A beret is the preferred hat of French peas Jean-Claude Pea and Phillipe Pea.

B

BENNY

B

best (BEST) Better than all else. Larry was the best tap dancer in the talent show.

Bethany (BETH-uh-nee) A town about two miles from Jerusalem on the southeastern slope of the Mount of Olives.

Bethel (BETH-ul) "House of God"; a city in Palestine, about 10 miles north of Jerusalem.

Bethesda, Pool of (beth-EZ-da) A pool with water that came from an underground spring. People thought the water would heal them and would try to be the first one in the water when it was stirred. Jesus healed a crippled man at the pool.

Bethlehem (BETH-luh-hem) The town where Jesus was born.

betray (be-TRAY) To be disloyal to someone. Little Joe was betrayed by his brothers in the video "The Ballad of Little Joe."

Bible (BY-bul) God's Word which is totally true. The Bible is divided into two main parts, the Old Testament and the New Testament.

bid (BID) To make an offer of or proposal for something.

Biggle-bag trees (BIG-ul BAG TREES) A luscious fruit-bearing tree found only in the land of Snoodleburg.

Bilhah (BIL-hah) The maid-servant to Jacob's wife Rachel.

bind (BYND) To tie up. See *Proverbs 6:21.*

birth (berth) The act or process of a baby being born. Junior celebrated the day of his birth by having a party with his family—that's what's called a birthday party!

bishop (BISH-up) A high-ranking leader of the church.

Bithynia (bith-IN-ee-ah) One of the stops in Paul's travels.

blame (BLAYM) To find fault with. See what Paul has to say about blame in *Philippians 2:15*. Bob tries not to blame Larry for everything that goes wrong!

blaspheme (BLAS-feem) To dishonor or be disrespectful to God.

bless (BLES) To honor during worship time; to express good wishes or offer prayers for.

blessed (BLES-id) or (BLEST) Wonderful; pleasing to God.

Jesus talks about how it is to be blessed in *Matthew 5:3–11*.

blessing (BLES-sing) A wonderful gift from God.

B

blossom (BLOS-sum) The flower of a plant. Larry discovered that blossom rhymes with opossum.

blue (BLOO) To be sad; a primary color. Madame Blueberry was so blue she didn't know what to do.

Blue Lobster (BLOO LOB-stur) Larry's toy; a wind-up blue-colored sea creature; a great name for a restaurant specializing in seafood.

BLUE LOBSTER

boast (BOAST) To show off and be prideful. See what Paul has to say about being boastful in *Ephesians 2:9*.

boat (BOAT) A vessel that floats on water.

Boaz (BO-az) In the Bible, the husband of Ruth.

BOB THE TOMATO

Bob the Tomato (BOB the toe-MAY-toe) A lovable, but serious Veggie who loves to teach kids about God.

bold (BOLD) Fearless and daring; courageous. See *Acts* 4:29. Edward was both strong and bold during the Great Pie Wars in "King George and The Ducky".

bon appétit (bone a-peh-TEET) The words for "good eating" in the French language. Do you know in which VeggieTales episode Mr. Nezzer says bon appétit?

bondage (BON-dadg) To be in captivity.

book of life A list of God's people. The Bible says that only the names that are in the book of life will go to heaven. See *Revelation 3:5*.

boot (BOOT) Protective footgear, often made of leather or rubber, covering the foot and part or all of the leg. A boot is worn by the Flibbians in Flibber-o-loo.

born (BORN) Coming into the world; to be born again is a term used to mean given new life through Christ and the Holy Spirit. See *John 3:3*.

borrow (BAR-oh) To take something with the promise of giving it back.

boss (BOSS) The person in charge at a place of work. Mr. Nezzer was the boss at the Chocolate Factory.

bother (BAH-ther) To pester. It really bothers Archibald Asparagus when Larry says that everyone has a water buffalo when everyone clearly does not have a water buffalo.

boulder (BOLD-er) A very large rock.

bounty (BOUN-tee) Abundant harvest.

bow (BOW) To bend the body at the waist as a show of respect. Rack, Shack, and Benny did not bow down to the 90-foot-tall chocolate bunny.

bowling (BOH-ling) A fun game involving knocking over ten pins with a ball (preferably a bowling ball). Junior's dad enjoyed bowling a whole bunch.

BOYZ IN THE SINK

Boyz in the Sink (BOIZ in the SINGK) The talented, all-boy band famous for "The Belly Button Song."

branches (BRAN-chez) Offspring limbs of a tree. Jesus talks about how he is the vine and we are the branches in *John 15:5*.

brave (BRAYV) Courageous. Jonah had to be brave when God asked him to go to Nineveh.

bread (BRED) A baked food usually made from flour with or without yeast.

B

break (BRAYK) To separate into parts; to shatter. See what the Bible says about breaking of bread in *Matthew 26:26.*

bridegroom (BRYD-groom). A man who is about to be married or is recently married.

broccoli (BRAH-kuh-lee) A green vegetable with a stalk and florets on the top. A real favorite with the kids! "Broccoli! Celery! Gotta be! VeggieTales!"

bronze (BRONZ) A mixture of copper and tin.

brother (BRUH-ther) A male having the same parents as another; a friend. David and Jonathan were such close friends, they were like brothers.

buddy (BUD-ee) A good friend whom you can count on. Bob is Larry's good buddy.

build (BILD) To put together or assemble; to encourage one another. Paul tried

BUNGEE, bungee, bungee-bungee-wungee

to build up the Thessalonians by telling them good news. See *1 Thessalonians 5:11.*

Bumblyburg (BUM-blee-burg) A friendly and peaceful little town, home to the crime-fighting, superhero cuke, Larryboy.

bungee (BUN-jee) An elastic cord used for absorbing shock. "Bungee, bungee, bungee-bungee-wungee!" What VeggieTales video is that from?

bunny (BUN-ee) A rabbit, especially a young one. "The bunny, the bunny, oh, I love the bunny."

burden (BUR-den) A load to carry. See *Galatians 6:2.* Junior Asparagus learned that fibbing can be a real burden.

Burger Bell (BUR-ger BELL) Mr. Lunt's favorite fast food restaurant, specializing in cheeseburgers, of course.

burn (BURN) Devoured by fire. "The people would burn sacrifices in honor of the Lord."

bury (BER-ee) To cover up.

business (BIZ-ness) The work a person does; a company. When proceeded by the word "monkey," business means "shenanigans," "goofin' around."

Buzz-Saw Louie (BUZZ-saw LOO-ee) A doll that knows the "true" meaning of Christmas. "You want a toy that's fun! You want a toy that's cute! You want Buzz-Saw Louie!"

BUZZ-SAW LOUIE

Caesar (SEE-zer) The emperor of Rome.

Caiaphas (KY-uh-fus) He was the high priest who planned to kill Jesus. See *John 18:13–14.*

Cain (KAYN) Oldest son of Adam and Eve, killed his brother, Abel.

Caleb (KAY-leb) One of the twelve spies Moses sent to find out about the Promised Land of Canaan. He and Joshua were the only two people who encouraged the people to go up and possess the land, and they alone were spared when a plague broke out in which the other ten spies perished.

Calvary (KAL-vuh-ree) The hill where Jesus was crucified.

camel (KA-mul) A hump-backed mammal that lives in arid, or dry, regions.

Jonah has a **CAMEL** instead of a car.

camp (KAMP) A collection of tents or buildings in close proximity for those who enjoy the outdoors. Abraham and Sarah lived in tents in a camp with all their family, servants, and animals.

Singing songs around a **CAMPFIRE**

campfire (KAMP-fy-ur) A fire set usually in a circle of stones, outside at campouts; a gathering spot for campers. A campfire is not a good place for a snowman.

Cana (KAY-nah) A town in Galilee where Jesus turned water into wine.

Canaan (KAY-nan) An ancient region made up of Palestine or the part between the Jordan River and the Mediterranean Sea; the

Promised Land of the Israelites.

canal (kuh-NAL) A waterway. In "The Wonderful World of Auto-tainment," Pa Grape sings a song about the most famous of all canals, the Erie Canal, in a song titled "Erie Canal."

canister set (KAN-ih-stur SET) Containers used to hold kitchen goods such as flour, sugar, or Madame Blueberry's sauces.

Capernaum (kah-PUR-nay-um) A city in Galilee where Jesus and his disciples often did teaching.

captain (KAP-tun) The person in charge of a boat crew. Pa Grape wears a captain's hat when he's one of the Pirates Who Don't Do Anything.

care (KAIR) Caution in avoiding harm or danger; thinking about others; helping others with their problems. See *John 21:16* where Jesus instructs Peter, "Take care of my sheep."

carpenter (KAR-pen-tur) Someone who makes things out of wood.

cash (KASH) Money in the form of coins and bills.

catapult (KAT-uh-pult) A machine to launch something into the air. With a catapult, you could launch a dodgeball, a rubber ducky, or mashed potatoes up against a wall!

cave (KAYV) An underground cavern.

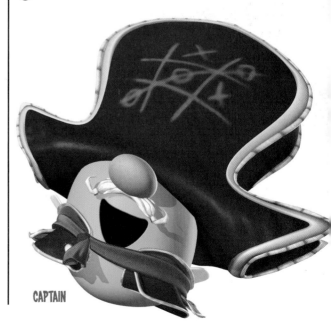

CAPTAIN

CAVIS APPYTHART

Cavis Appythart (KA-vis AP-pee-thart) Cavis is a recurring character played by Bob the Tomato, first seen in "The Star of Christmas," then in "An Easter Carol."

cebú (say-BOO) According to Larry, it's kind of like a cow, but not a water buffalo.

celebrate (SEL-uh-brayt) To observe a holiday, perform a religious ceremony, or take part in a festival. The towns-people sure did celebrate when the church was saved in "An Easter Carol."

celery (sel-u-rE) An herb related to the carrot because of the thick edible stems of its leaves. Laura Carrot, however, is very different from Frankencelery. And Frankencelery, although sounding a little scary, is really an actor from Toledo named Phil Winklestein.

census (SEN-sus) An effort to get a complete count of a population. Mary and Joseph traveled to Bethlehem to take part in the census.

centurion (sen-TEEUR-ee-un) A high-ranking commanding officer in the Roman army.

Cephas (SEE-fuss) Jesus gave this name to the apostle Simon, who later became know as Simon Peter. In *John 1:42*, Jesus names Peter Cephas, which means, "rock."

ceremony (SAIR-uh-moh-nee) A formal party.

chair (CHAIR) A piece of furniture used for sitting on. Archibald Asparagus likes to lounge in a chair to read books.

challenge (CHAL-uhnj) To call out to duel or combat. When Jonah challenged God's command, he ended up in the belly of a whale.

THE CHAMPION.
Apollo Gourd

champion (CHAM-pee-un) The winner of a challenge or contest. In "Sumo of the Opera," the Italian Scallion challenges Apollo Gourd for the title of World Veggie-Weight Champion.

change (CHAYNJ) To alter, adjust, or correct something. "Unless you change and become like little children, you will never enter the kingdom of heaven." See *Matthew 18:3*.

character (KAIR-ak-ter) The way one acts because of who he is on the inside. In *Galatians 5:22–23*, the Bible tells us the traits of good character.

chariot (CHAIR-ee-ut) A device that carries a driver behind a horse or horses.

CHEESEBURGER.

cheeseburger (CHEEZ-bur-gur) A burger topped with a piece of cheese. Mr. Lunt sings: "'Cuz he loves you cheeseburger with all his heart, and there's nothin' gonna tear you two apart . . .'"

C

C

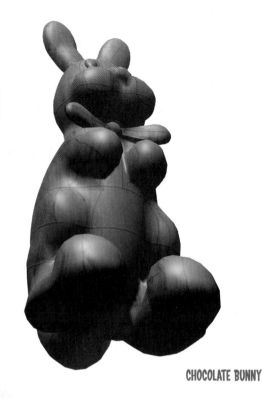

CHOCOLATE BUNNY

cherubim (CHAIR-uh-bim) Heavenly beings with wings and faces of men and animals that guarded the Garden of Eden.

chief priest (CHEEF PREEST) The highest ranking priest/religious leader.

children (CHIL-drun) Young people who are wonderful gifts from heaven! "Jesus said, 'Let the little children come to me . . .'" See *Matthew 19:14.*

chocolate bunny (CHAWK-uh-let BUN-ee) A sweet confection in the shape of a rabbit made in Mr. Nezzer's factory in "Rack, Shack, and Benny"; they are enjoyed by children at Easter time.

Chocolate Factory (CHAWK-uh-let FAK-tuh-ree) The Veggie factory where chocolate bunnies are made and managed by the greedy Mr. Nezzer in "Rack, Shack, and Benny."

choose (CHOOZ) To make a choice or decision. "You did not choose me, but I chose you . . ." See *John 15:16.*

chore (CHOAR) A job to do.

chorus (KOR-us) The main part of a song that is often repeated. In the "Yodeling Veterinarian of the Alps," the chorus is: Yodel-leh-hee yodel-leh-hee yodel-leh-hoo. Yodel-leh-hee yodel-leh-hee yodel-eee-ooo. Yodel-leh-hee yodel-leh-hee yodel-leh-hoo. Yada-yada yada-yada yad-eee-ooo!

Christ (KRYST) The Messiah, as foretold by the prophets of the Hebrew Scriptures; Jesus.

Christian (KRIS-chun) Someone who belongs to the family of Christ because they believe that Jesus died on the cross for their sins.

Christmas (KRIS-mus) The holiday celebrating Jesus' birth.

1 Chronicles (FURST KRAHN-ih-culs) The thirteenth book of the Bible; written for the exiles,

A **CITIZEN** of Bumblyburg

reminds them that they are still God's chosen people.

2 Chronicles (SEK-und KRAHN-ih-culs) The fourteenth book of the Bible; continues sharing King David's royal family.

church (CHURCH) A house where Christians gather to praise God and learn about him; God's house; a great place to be with others. Paul teaches in *Acts 20:28*, "Be shepherds of the church of God . . ."

chute (SHOOT) An inclined passage down or through which things may pass. A Snoodle drops out of a chute on every fourth Tuesday night.

citizen (SIT-uh-zun) A member of a city, town, or state. Larryboy is a citizen of Bumblyburg.

city (SIT-ee) A place where people live that is bigger than a village or a town. Madame Blueberry liked to go into the city to buy more stuff.

climb (KLYM) To go upward with gradual or continuous progress. There once was a man who climbed over a hill and came down with all the bananas.

coconut (KOH-kuh-nut) A hard, round, hairy fruit with a yummy fruit and milk in the inside. A coconut is not a good thing to use as a bowling ball.

Colosse (kuh-LAH-see) The town that held one of the earliest churches.

Colossians (kuh-LAH-shuns) The seventh book of letters in the New Testament, written by Paul to help the people of Colosse keep their church strong.

collard greens (KAHL-urd GREENS) A vegetable in the cabbage family with loose leaves connected to a stalk. They are not actually found wearing collars.

colt (KOHLT) A young male horse. Jesus rode on a colt. See *Matthew 21:2*.

comfort (KUHM-furt) To soothe in time of affliction or distress. See *Psalm 23:4* for how God comforts us when we're scared.

command (kuh-MAND) To give an order to. Mr. Nezzer commanded all his factory workers to bow down to the bunny.

commandment (kuh-MAND-ment) An order that has been made by someone; God's laws were given to Moses for all God's people in this format. See *Exodus 20:1–17* to learn about the commandments God gave to Moses.

commend (kuh-MEND) To express approval of; praise. When Junior admitted that his father's Art Bigotti collector's plate had been broken, his father commended him for telling the truth.

commit (kuh-MIT) To put in trust or charge; entrust. Before you commit your pet to the care of the yodeling veterinarian of the Alps, you may want to get a second opinion.

communication (kuh-myoo-ni-KAY-shun) The act of sharing information. Bob and Larry have communication with kids by sharing God's stories in a fun way.

communion (KUH-myoon-yun) A Christian sacrament in which bread and wine are taken in remembrance of Jesus. The bread reminds us of his body. The wine reminds us of his blood.

community (kuh-MYOON-ih-tee) A group of people who live in a certain area. The community that resides in Snoodleburg is made up of curious folks who are said to eat pancakes with their noodles.

companion (kuhm-PAN-yun) A friend who often travels with you. Khalil was Jonah's traveling companion.

compassion (kuhm-PASH-un) What you feel for others when you show loving concern for them and want to show them kindness. "Clothe yourselves with compassion, kindness, humility, gentleness and patience." See *Colossians 3:12*. According to Pa Grape, compassion is when you see people who need help and you want to help them.

compel (kuhm-PEL) To try to force something to happen.

Madame Blueberry likes to **COMPLAIN.**

complain (kuhm-PLAIN) To grumble; to express unhappiness about something. Madame Blueberry liked to complain a lot to her butlers.

C

COMPUTER

computer (kuhm-PEW-ter) A piece of equipment used for processing information. Qwerty is the computer that Bob and Larry use to get Bible verses in VeggieTales.

concern (kuhn-SURN) Interest in, or wanting to care for any person or thing.

condemn (kuhn-DEM) To pronounce judgment against.

confess (kuhn-FES) To admit to doing something wrong.

confidence (KAHN-fuh-dens) Feeling very sure about something. Larry shows he has a lot of confidence by being one cool cucumber in the Silly Song, "The Dance of the Cucumber."

conscience (KAHN-shuns) When you are overwhelmed with the right thing to do. Lyle let his conscience be his guide in "Lyle, the Kindly Viking."

conspire (kuhn-SPY-ur) To make a secret plot.

consume (kun-soom) To destroy completely, as if by fire; to use up; to eat a lot of. Jimmy and Jerry Gourd like to consume large amounts of food.

content (kuhn-TENT) To be happy with the way things are. The Pirates Who Don't Do Anything are content with ping pong and cheese curls.

control (KON-trol) To keep within limits; to have power over.

conversion (kun-VER-zhun) A decision to make a change and turn completely to God. In *Acts* you can read about the conversions of Paul and of many others.

An Easter Egg **CONVEYOR BELT**

conveyor belt (kuhn-VAY-er BELT) A machine used to move objects from place to place. A conveyor belt is found in factories like Wally Nezzer's toy factory and his brother Nebby K. Nezzer's chocolate factory.

convict (KAHN-vict) A prisoner who broke the law. Mr. Pincher is a convict in "The Star of Christmas."

Corinth (KOR-inth) One of the first places that Paul developed the early church.

1 Corinthians (FURST kor-IN-thee-uns) The second book of letters in the New Testament, written by Paul to the people struggling to obey God's will in Corinth.

2 Corinthians (SEK-und kor-IN-thee-uns) The third book of letters in the New Testament, written by Paul to the people in Corinth a few months after he sent the first letter because things weren't getting any better. It is a book on both sadness and joy.

cornerstone (kor-ner-STONE) An important stone in the corner of a building. The cornerstone had to be perfect so the walls would be straight.

C

council (KOWN-sel)   A group of people who meet to discuss laws and the defense of people who broke the laws. In biblical times, it was called the "Sanhedrin," the highest Jewish court.

counselor (KOWN-sul-ur) Someone who gives advice; another name for God as he sends the Holy Spirit to help us.

courage (KUHR-ij) To be very brave. "Be on your guard; stand firm in the faith; be men of courage; be strong. Do everything in love." See *1 Corinthians 16:13–14.* When Esther knows she has to make an important decision, she prays to God, and finds the courage to do what's right.

courtyard (kO(o)rt yärd) The part of a building that has walls but no roof.

covenant (KUH-vuh-nent) A promise that two people make between one another. See *Luke 22:14–20* to see how Jesus talked about covenants at the Last Supper.

COVET a ducky.

covet (KUHV-it) To want something that someone else has. One of the Ten Commandments says not to covet anything that belongs to someone else. See *Exodus 20:17.* King George coveted Thomas' ducky, even though he had an entire cabinet full of his own.

coward (KOW-urd) Someone who is too frightened to do something.

create (kree-AYT) To make, build, or construct something new or original. God created everything!

creation (kree-AY-shun) The act of God bringing the entire world into existence. "In the beginning God created the heavens and the earth." *See Genesis 1:1.*

creator (kre-ATE-er) God, the maker of heaven and earth.

crime (KRYM) The act of breaking the law. Greta Von Gruesome, evil ruler of Zuchinia, committed the crime of kidnapping the world's greatest yodelers.

criminal (KRIM-uh-nul) Someone who has broken the law. Awful Alvin is a criminal who likes to dance with Lampy.

crippled (KRI-pulled) Someone who is injured or disabled so that he or she cannot walk.

cross (KRAWS) The upright post with an intersection piece upon which Jesus was crucified. *See John 19:17.*

crown (KROWN) A beautiful circle worn on the head by royalty. "You will receive the crown of glory that will never fade away." *See 1 Peter 5:4.*

crucify (KROO-sih-fy) The act of nailing someone to a cross that results in their death. Jesus was crucified for our sins. *See Luke 23:33.*

cruel (KROO-ul) Causing emotional or physical hurt to others; being unkind. Bob and Larry teach kids that God doesn't want us to be cruel to others.

cry (KRY) To be sad or in pain and have tears fall from your eyes. Madame Blueberry cried a lot because she didn't think she had enough stuff.

Madame Blueberry **CRIED** a lot.

C
D

Larry is
a **CUCUMBER.**

cucumber (KEYEOO-kuhm-bur) A long, round fruit that has a green rind and crisp white flesh, often mistaken for a vegetable. Larry is one of them!

curious (KYOOR-EE-us) Wanting to learn new things.

custom (KUHS-tum) A tradition. Many years ago, the people of Flibber-o-loo made it a custom to wear on their heads one large shoe.

customer (KUHS-tuh-mur) Someone who shops in a store. The Stuff-Mart has many loyal customers who buy lots of stuff there.

Damascus (Duh-MAS-cus) Town where Saul was healed and became a believer.

dance (DANS) To move your body to the beat of a song; to express yourself in artful praise to God. "The Dance of the Cucumber" is a very silly Silly Song.

Daniel (DAN-yul) A man in the Bible who had great faith and trusted in God; was not harmed when he was thrown in a lions' den.

David (DAY-vid) Jesse's son; chosen by God to be the second king of Israel.

deacon (DEE-kun) A worker in the church.

Dead Sea (DED SEE) This is a very large lake found on the south side of the Jordan River; also known as the Salt Sea or the Sea of Arabah.

death (DEHTH) The end of life. "Jesus gave them this answer: 'I tell you the truth, . . . whoever hears my word and believes him who sent me has eternal life and will not be condemned; he has crossed over from death to life.'" See *John 5:19–24*.

Deborah (DEB-uh-rah) A judge and prophet who aided the Israelites in their victory over the Canaanites.

debt (det) An amount of money, service, or gratitude, that is owed to someone else. Paul tells us in *Romans 13:8* to not have any debt except the dept to love one another.

decide (dee-SYD) To make a final choice.

decision (dih-SIZH-un) A final choice that is made.

Junior Asparagus made the decision to eat chocolate chip cookies rather than anchovies.

declare (dih KLAR) To orally make known; to state publicly.

decree (dih-KREE) Laws that are made; an official decision of the emperor. King Darius made a decree that anyone who prayed to God should be thrown in a den of lions. Daniel broke the decree by praying to God and he was put in the lions' den. See *Daniel 6*.

dedicate (ded-i-KATE) To offer or set aside for someone; to donate or give something to someone; to commit yourself to someone.

defeat (dih-FEET) To win victory over. Larry thinks it's those funny things we put into shoes. Is he right?

deity (DE-et-E) Someone who is worshiped; supremely good or powerful, like a god.

D

Delilah (dee-LYE-luh) She was a Philistine woman whom Samson was in love with. She tricked Samson into revealing his secret strength, which caused him to betray God.

deliver (dih-LIV-ur) To hand over someone or something to another. "I sought the LORD, and he answered me; he delivered me from all my fears." See *Psalm 34:4.* As God's messenger, Jonah's job was to deliver the Word of God.

demon (DEE-mun) An evil spirit.

descend (dee-SEND) To go from a higher place to a lower one. "At that moment heaven was opened, and he saw the Spirit of God descending like a dove and lighting on him." See *Matthew 3:16.*

descendants (dee-SEN-dants) Members of a family who are born from one generation to another.

A desert of **DESSERT**

desert (DEZ-ert) A very hot, dry region of land. After 40 years of wandering in the desert, the children of Israel finally get to go to the Promised Land!

deserve (dee-SERV) To be worthy of. No one deserves to go to heaven, but Jesus died so that we could go to heaven. See *John 3:16.*

desire (dee-SYR) To long or hope for; to want to do something. It was Junior's desire to watch the television program with Frankencelery in it.

dessert (dee-ZERT) A yummy, good-to-eat treat after a meal; a word that often gets confused with desert.

destroy (dih-STROY) To ruin completely.

destruction (dih-STRUK-shun) The act of destroying.

Deuteronomy (doo-tur-ON-uh-mee) The fifth book of the Old Testament; written by Moses about God's laws and his love.

devil (DEH-vul) The supreme spirit of evil.

Junior **DESIRES** to watch TV.

devote (di-VOTE) To commit to, to determine to use something for a particular purpose. After Paul was saved, he devoted his whole life to preaching about Christ.

difficulty (DIF-uh-kul-tee) Something not easily done, understood, or solved. Bob the tomato has difficulty riding a bike because he can't reach the pedals.

Dinah (DY-nah) Joseph's sister.

Dinkletown (DING-kul-toun) The Veggie town in which "The Toy That Saved Christmas" is set.

disciple (dih-SY-pul) Someone who is a follower and believer of their chosen leader. Jesus had twelve close disciples, and he calls all of us to be his disciples. "Therefore go and make disciples of all nations, baptizing them in the name of the Father and of the Son and of the Holy Spirit . . ." See *Matthew 28:19*.

discipline (DIH-sih-plin) To train or develop by instruction and exercise. "Discipline your son, for in that there is hope . . ." See *Proverbs 19:18*.

D

disease (dih-ZEEZ) A serious illness.

disgrace (dis-GRAYS) To lose honor.

Larry's wearing a **DISGUISE**.

disguise (dis-GYZ) To mask or change the way someone looks. Like any good superhero worth his weight in kidney pies, Larryboy has an excellent disguise, complete with super-suction ears.

dishonest (dis-ON-est) To lie; to be deceitful. "Do not use dishonest standards when measuring length, weight or quantity." See *Leviticus 19:35*. Junior was dishonest when he told a fib about the broken plate.

dismayed (dis-MADE) To be disappointed in something; shock, panic, or sadness in a situation.

disobey (dis-oh-BAY) To refuse to follow a command or instruction. Jonah disobeyed God's command and ended up inside a whale's belly.

dizzy (DIZ-ee) When your head feels faint and wobbly and you think you may fall over. Watching Snoodle Doo fly around Snoodleburg could make you dizzy.

Dodgeball City (DAHJ BAWL SIH-tee) The Veggie town that Little Joe settles in.

Dorcas (DOR-kus) This was a Christian woman who helped the poor. She was also known by the name Tabitha. See *Acts 9:36*.

doubt (DOUT) An uncertainty; not having confidence in; a possible distrust or suspicion about something. Jesus told Thomas to stop doubting him. See *John 20:27.*

dove (DUV) The bird that was mentioned as a sign of the Holy Spirit in *Matthew 3:16*; it was also the type of bird that returned to Noah to show him that the land was dry in *Genesis 8:11.*

Larry has a **DREAM** when he sleeps.

dream (DREEM) The amazing thoughts and stories your brain has while your body is asleep. After watching scary movies, Junior was worried he would have scary dreams when he fell asleep.

drought (DROUT) Lack of rain or water; a long period of dry weather.

dungeon (DUN-jen) A dark underground prison. Worse than an ordinary prison, it was a more severe place of punishment.

duty (DOO-tee) A moral or legal obligation; a responsibility; a job. Larry felt it was his duty to take care of the dust bunnies under his bed; so he named them, fed them and played with them every day.

dwell (DWELL) To live inside of; to be a part of. "Let the word of Christ dwell in you richly as you teach and admonish one another..." See *Colossians 3:16.*

dwelling (DWEL-ing) A house or a shelter. Madame Blueberry's dwelling is on top of a tree, so it is called a tree house.

D

eager (EE-gur) To be willing or anxious to do something. Paul talks about being eager to serve God in *2 Corinthians 8:11-12.* Bob and Larry are eager to tell kids about God's stories in the Bible.

eagle (EE-gul) A magnificent bird of great speed and mighty strength, often used in the Bible to teach lessons. "But those who hope in the LORD . . . will soar on wings like eagles." See *Isaiah 40:31.*

ear muffs (EAR-mufs) Protective covering worn to keep ears warm. (Do not confuse these with English muffins. You may get butter on your ears.) In "The Toy That Saved Christmas," the young Veggies wore ear muffs to keep their ears warm while sledding.

earn (URN) To be paid for something; to do some-thing worthy of something in return.

earth (URTH) The planet that we live on; a beautiful round sphere in the universe that God created.

earthquake (URTH-kwake) A trembling and shaking of the earth. See *Matthew 27:54* to learn about the earth-quake that happened at the time of Jesus' death.

Easter (EE-stur) The joyous holiday celebrating Jesus' resurrection; a time of rebirth and renewal.

EAR MUFFS

EBENEZER K. NEZZER

Ebenezer K. Nezzer (eh-ben-EEZ-er KAY NEH-zer) A zucchini Veggie character related to Nebby P. Nezzer. He was in "An Easter Carol" and learned the true message of what Easter means. See *Luke 24.*

Ecclesiastes (ee-klee-zee-AS-tees) The twenty-first book of the Old Testament, filled with poetry and wisdom; tells us to keep our lives centered on God.

Eden, Garden of (EE-den) The beautiful place where God created Adam and Eve and everything was perfect.

EDMUND

Edmund (ED-mund) A Veggie character played by Junior Asparagus in "The Star of Christmas" and "An Easter Carol"; he is the pastor's son at St. Bart's Church.

effort (EFF-urt) Trying hard. "Make every effort to live in peace with all men and to be holy . . ." See *Hebrews 12:14.* Esther made an effort to help her people.

Egypt (EE-jipt) A country in the northeast continent of Africa. Moses led the Israelites out of Egypt to the Promised Land.

elders (EL-derz) A special group of men who were leaders of God's people. Elders had authority to lead the church. In the New Testament, elders are also called "pastors" or "overseers."

ELECTRICIAN

electrician (ee-lec-TRIH-shun) Skilled worker who is good at connecting electric wires. Madame Blueberry asked Larry the Cucumber to install a light outside her treehouse since he is the only licensed electrician in Bumblyburg.

Eli (EE-lie) High priest and judge of Israel who raised Samuel.

Eliab (ee-LEE-ab) David's oldest brother.

Elijah (ee-LY-jah) A Hebrew prophet in the Old Testament who spoke for God and taught that we are not to worship idols.

Elisha (ee-LYSH-ah) A prophet who came after Elijah, performed miracles for God, and provided messages from God to his people.

Elizabeth (ee-LIZ-ah-beth) Mother of John the Baptist and cousin to Mary, the mother of Jesus.

Emmaus (ee-MAY-us) The city the two disciples were traveling to when Jesus appeared to them right after he rose from the dead. See *Luke 24:13–35* to learn more about what the disciples did when Jesus appeared to them on the road to Emmaus.

employee (em-PLOY-ee) Someone who works for someone else. Rack, Shack, and Benny were Mr. Nezzer's employees at his chocolate factory.

empty (EMP-tee) Not filled; vacant; without stuff inside, be it grape juice, candy, or Snooberry Jell-O®.

encourage (en-KUR-ij) To inspire with courage, spirit, or hope. "Therefore encourage one another and build each other up, just as in fact you are doing." See *1 Thessalonians 5:11*.

endure (en-DYOOR) To suffer through something without giving up. Read about how endurance "is commendable before God." See *1 Peter 2:20*. Thomas had to endure getting pelted by a variety of gooey pies in "King George and the Ducky."

enemy (EN-ih-mee) Someone or something that wants to cause you harm. Satan is the enemy of Jesus.

enter (EN-tur) To go in. The Italian Scallion entered the wrestling ring in "Sumo of the Opera."

An **ENTIRE** Mr. Twisty's Bag

entire (en-TYR) The whole of; complete; total. I am so hungry I could eat an entire bag of Mr. Twisty's cheese curls all by myself.

E

envy (EN-vee) Wanting something someone else has; to be jealous of; to resent someone for having something you do not. See why you shouldn't be envious in *James 3:14-16*. Madame Blueberry envied her neighbors because they had stuff she didn't have.

Epaphras (EP-ah-fras) Man who brought the gospel to Colosse; possible founder of the Colossian church who encouraged Paul to write his letter.

Ephesians (ee-FEE-zhuns) The fifth book of letters in the New Testament, written by Paul, focusing on our relationships with other people.

Ephesus (EF-ih-sus) An ancient city of Greek Asia Minor where Paul preached.

Ephraim (EH-frah-im) Joseph's second-born son.

equal (EE-kwul) Having the same quantity or value as another. God's love is equal toward everyone.

Esau (EE-saw) He was the older son of Isaac and Rebekah who sold his birthright to his twin brother, Jacob, for a pot of stew.

escape (eh-SKAPE) To run or get away from; to flee. Paul escaped from Damascus by being lowered in a basket over a wall. See *Acts 9*.

ESTHER

Esther (ES-tur) The seventeenth book of the Old Testament; named after the Jewish girl who was chosen by King Xerxes, of Persia, to be his wife. Esther is a veggie character who teaches us to have courage to do what's right.

eternal (ee-TUR-nul) Lasts forever; endless. "God has given us eternal life, and this life is in his Son." See *1 John 5:11.*

eternal life (ee-TUR-nul LIFE) A new life in heaven that will never end, promised to those who believe in and follow Jesus.

Ethiopia (E-the-O-pe-a) A country in Africa that was situated south of Egypt.

Euphrates (yoo-FRAY-tees) A river in Egypt that helps define the border of the land promised to Abraham.

evangelist (ee-VAN-jel-ist) Someone who shares the gospel of Jesus. See *2 Timothy 4:1–5* where Paul describes how to teach others about Jesus.

Eve (EEV) The very first woman to be created by God; wife of Adam.

everlasting (EV-er-las-ting) Eternal, eternal life above. Something that will never die or end. God sent a rain-bow as a sign of his everlasting promise to never again flood the entire earth. See *Genesis 9:16.*

evidence (EV-i-dens) Proof or a sign that something is true; facts.

evil (EE-vul) Morally bad or wrong; wicked.

exalt (eg-ZALT) To lift up in praise. "Glorify the LORD with me; let us exalt his name together." See *Psalm 34:3.*

examine (eg-ZAM-in) To check something very carefully. Jimmy Gourd wants to examine the menu to see if they have any pepperoni pancakes.

example (eg-ZAM-pul) Something that is a representative of; a model of something. A good example of a sumo wrestler is Apollo Gourd.

exile (EG-zile) To force a person or group of people to leave and stay away from their own country, usually for political or religious reasons.

Exodus (EK-suh-dus) The second book of the Old Testament which includes the story of Moses and the Ten Commandments.

experience (ek-SPEAR-ee-ens) To have knowledge, skill, and practice in something; the ability to lead others because of the knowledge or skills aquired.

EXTINGUISH

extinguish (ex-TING-gwish) To end something or put something out.

Ezekiel (ee-ZEEK-yel) The twenty-sixth book of the Old Testament; Ezekiel was a prophet who urged the people to recommit their lives to God.

Ezra (EZ-rah) The fifteenth book of the Old Testament; tells the story of rebuilding the temple. Ezra was also a person who led a group of Israelites in how to worship God.

fail (FAYL) To not succeed at something. Read *Proverbs 15:22* to see how plans can fail or succeed. Until he met his Creator, Snoodle Doo thought he failed at just about everything he tried to do.

fair (FAIR) Just, unbiased, observing the rules. Bob and Larry decided that it was a fair idea if they were fair to one another, and it worked out fairly well.

faith (FAYTH) Belief, confidence, and trust in; belief in God. "Now faith is being sure of what we hope for and certain of what we do not see." See *Hebrews 11:1*. When you have faith, all things are possible, even battling giants, like Goliath.

faithful (FAYTH-ful) Loyal and devoted to someone or something; trustworthy. Christians are faithful followers of Jesus.

faithfulness (FAYTH-ful-ness) Full of faith, especially in God; being loyal and obedient to God.

fall (FALL) This word is sometimes used to describe the first sin committed by Adam and Eve.

false (FAWLS) Something that is not true; fake; incorrect. See *Matthew 7:15* to read about false prophets that come in sheep's clothing. Saying that your shoe tastes like bacon would, hopefully, be false.

family (FAM-uh-lee) All the members of a household; relatives; descendants.

famine (FAM-in) A food shortage. See *Genesis 41:25–31* to learn about the famine in the time of Joseph and his family. The town is having a famine; not even so much as a speck of Snooberry Jell-O® can be found.

famous (FAY-mus) Well known or legendary. Twippo is a famous singer in "Jonah, a VeggieTales Movie."

far-lilly bushes/flowers (FAR-lih-lee BU-shes/FLOU-urs) A beautiful flowering plant found in Snoodleburg.

farmer (FARM-er) The person who runs and maintains a farm.

Snoodle
FARMER

F

fasting (FAS-ting) Not eating; going without food for a purpose of dedication or concentration. Read about fasting in *Matthew 6:16–18.*

Junior's
FATHER

father (FAH-ther) A man who has a child; another name for God. My father's name was Al who is a chemical engineer that likes badminton, beets, and a horse named Beetle Bomb.

fathom (FATH-um) A unit of length equal to six feet (about 1.8 meters) used especially for measuring the depth of water.

fault (FAWLT) An error, mistake, or an oversight. A weakness or shortcoming in someone. The Italian Scallion's greatest fault was that he never finished what he started.

favor (FAY-vur) Something nice done for someone in order to help him out; to be looked upon with respect and kindness. Read about how Mary found favor with God in *Luke 1:30–31.*

fear (FEER) To be afraid of something; to worry. *Psalm 56:3* talks about how we don't have to fear when God is with us.

feast (FEEST) A large, celebratory meal. At Thanksgiving, it is customary to have a feast of turkey, mashed potatoes, stuffing, and pumpkin pie.

fellowship (FEL-oh-ship) A group of friends who share something in common such as their faith. "But if we walk in the light, as he is in the light, we have fellowship with one another . . ." See *1 John 1:7*.

fiery (FY-ur-ee) On fire or having fire all around. Shadrach, Meshach, and Abednego were put into a fiery furnace, but were not hurt. See *Daniel 3*. Rack, Shack, and Benny came face to face with a fiery furnace but chose to stand up for their beliefs.

fight (FITE) To struggle physically, verbally, or emotionally for something or with someone; a combat; a battle. The Italian Scallion chose to fight Apollo Gourd in a wrestling match.

find (FYND) To see or discover something after look-ing for it. A good way to find someone whom God loves very much is to look into a mirror.

firstborn (FIRST-born) The first child born in a family. Read about Mary's firstborn son, Jesus, in *Luke 2:6–7*.

fish (PHISH) A cold-blooded creature of the sea with fins and gills. Before they met Jesus, Simon and Andrew caught fish for a living.

fish-slappers (FISH-SLA-pers) Veggie characters who represented the Ninevites from the Bible and went around slapping people with smelly, old fishes.

flee (FLEE) To run away or escape.

Flibber-o-loo (FLIH-bur-oh-loo) A town whose inhabitants wear shoes on their heads.

float (FLOTE) Staying on top of the water.

F

F

The Rumor
Weed can
FLOURISH.

flock (FLOK) A gathering or collection of something such as sheep. Shepherds watched their flocks at night. The kids in their crazy hairdos flocked to the Flock of Seagulls concert.

flogged (FLAHGD) Beaten or whipped.

flood (FLUD) An overabundance of water. See *Genesis 7* to learn what happened when God flooded the earth.

flourish (FLUR-ish) To grow and do well. With every rumor successfully planted, the Rumor Weed flourished and spread.

follower (FAH-lo-wur) Someone who follows another; someone who is devoted to, pursues, or goes after another. Jesus had twelve close followers who became his disciples.

foolish (FOOL-ish) Unwise. See *Matthew 25:1–13* to see how Jesus taught about being foolish in a parable. It is foolish to try to make ice in a sauna.

footwashing (FOOT-washing) Showing honor to someone by washing their feet. See *John 13:2–17* where Jesus washed his disciples' feet.

forbid (for-BID) To not allow. The parents of the child forbid him to paint daisies on the big, red rubber ball.

forefathers (for-FAHTH-urs) People in a family who lived earlier in time.

foreign (FOR-in) From a different country; something or someone unknown. See *Hebrews 11:9* where God leads Abraham to a foreign country.

forever (for-EV-ur) A time that does not end; eternal. Christians will live in heaven forever.

forgive (for-GIV) To excuse someone who has done something wrong; to pardon or let off the hook. "Forgive us our debts, as we also have forgiven our debtors." See *Matthew 6:12.* Junior tried to forgive the Grapes of Wrath, even though they were mean to him.

forsake (for-SAKE) To abandon or leave behind.

fortress (FOR-tres) A well-protected shelter or castle. The corn dog stand provided a great fortress on the beach.

fortune (FOR-chun) Wealth, riches, and treasure.

foundation (foun-DAY-shun) An underlying base or support. Faith in God gives life a solid foundation. See *2 Timothy 2:19*

fragile (FRA-jul) Something very breakable; something weak or frail. An Art Bigotti Collector's Plate is a very fragile thing.

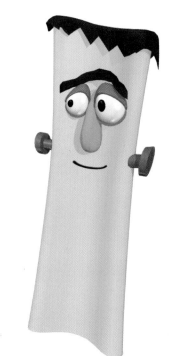

FRANKENCELERY

Frankencelery (FRANK-ken-sel-ree) A Veggie character and actor from Toledo, whose real name is Phil Winkelstein. He stars in a scary movie that Junior Asparagus watches before going to bed.

frankincense (fran-kin-SENSE) A natural product burned to make pleasant aroma, often referred to as incense. One of the gifts the wise men brought to Jesus was frankincense. See *Matthew 2:11.*

free (FREE) Not requiring payment; limitless or uncontrolled.

A FRENCH PEA

French Peas (FRENCH PEES) Clever, hard-working Veggies from France; they go by the names of Jean-Claude and Phillipe Pea.

friend (FREND) Somebody that you spend time with and can depend on. "A friend loves at all times . . ." See *Proverbs 17:17.* Junior and Laura are good friends.

fruit (FROOT) The edible part of a seed plant. A Biggle-bag tree grows a nice fruit.

Fruit of the Spirit (FROOT of the SPIH-rit) Love, joy, peace, patience, kindness, goodness, faithfulness, gentleness, self-control. See *Galatians 5:22–23.*

frustration (frus-TRAY-shun) Irritation or unhappiness about something. Bob felt a great deal of frustration with Larry when Larry would not listen to him.

fulfill (ful-FIL) To accomplish; satisfy, bring to a successful end. With his school duties fulfilled, Maewyn Succat returned to Ireland to teach the Druids about God.

funny (FUN-ee) Something that makes you laugh. Silly Songs are funny!

Larry of the **FUTURE**

furnace (FUR-nis) A big machine that creates and generates heat for a building. A furnace is not a nice place to put three upstanding lads like Rack, Shack, and Benny.

fury (FYUR-e) Violent anger and rage.

future (FYU-chur) What is yet to come; the outlook or expectation down the road. See *Romans 8:38–39* to be reminded how nothing in the future can separate us from "the love of God that is in Christ Jesus our Lord."

F
G

Gabriel (GAY-bree-el) The angel that appeared to Jesus' mother.

Gad (GAD) Joseph's brother.

gain (GAYN) Increase; grow. See what Paul has to say about gain in *Philippians 1:21–26*.

Galatia (ga-LAY-shuh) One of the stops in Paul's travels.

Galatians (ga-LAY-shuns) The fourth book of letters in the New Testament is written by Paul to encourage the people of Galatia as they developed their churches.

Galilee (GAL-ih-lee) A strong early church region.

garden (GAR-dun) A lovely, fertile place where plants grow, some bearing fruit and vegetables, some bearing flowers.

Garden of Eden The home God created for Adam and Eve where they named the animals and talked with God. When Adam and Eve sinned, they had to leave the Garden of Eden. Read about it in *Genesis 2*.

garment (GAR-ment) A piece of clothing.

gather (GA-thur) To bring things together. The Veggies like to gather at the countertop.

geneology (JEE-nee-ahl-o-gee) A list off one's ancestors.

generation (jen-er-A-shon) The amount of time it takes for people to grow up and have their own children; about thirty-eight years.

generous (JEN-ur-us) Regularly giving or sharing. "Good will comes to him who is generous and lends freely . . . " See *Psalm 112:5*.

Genesis (JEN-ih-sis) The very first book of the Bible that focuses on many beginnings.

genius (JEEN-yus) Someone who is very smart or has supreme intelligence. The Silly Song, "I Love My Lips" must have been created by a genius!

Gentiles (JEN-tiles) In Bible times, the Jews called anyone who was not a Jew a Gentile; a word that means "nations." The Jews thought these people were their enemies. But Jesus taught a different message, inviting both the

Jews and the Gentiles into a relationship with God.

gentle (JEN-tul) Very mild or delicate; calm; tender. "A gentle answer turns away wrath, but a harsh word stirs up anger." See *Proverbs 15:1.*

gentleness (JEN-tul-ness) Kind, soft, and soothing; calm.

Gethsemane (Geth-SEM-uh-nee) The garden where Jesus prayed, at the foot of the Mount of Olives.

giant (JI-ent) A person who is unusually tall and large. Goliath was around nine feet, four inches tall. Dave knew that with God's help, little guys could do big things too. So he was willing to face the giant, Goliath. From "Dave and the Giant Pickle."

Gideon (GID-ee-un) A Hebrew judge who opposed the Baal cult and defeated the Midianites.

gift (GIFT) A present given from the heart; a talent or ability. "For it is by grace you have been saved . . . it is the gift of God . . ." See *Ephesians 2:8-9.* All the children wanted a Buzz-Saw Louie doll for a gift at Christmas.

G

Larry's all wrapped up like a **GIFT.**

Gilead (GIL-ee-ad) A region in Bible times that many fugitives fled to.

give (GIV) To offer something to someone freely. *Larry offered to give Bob his collection of candy wrappers.*

glad (GLAD) Content; pleased.

glorious (GLOR-ee-us) Something magnificent or wonderful. Read *1 Peter 1:8* to hear about how believing in Jesus fills you with glorious joy.

glory (GLOR-ee) Adoration, praise, and thanksgiving offered in worship.

glutton (GLUH-tun) One who wants food in excess amounts.

gnat (NAT) A tiny, flying bug.

goat (GOTE) A farm animal that says "maaa" and likes to eat everything in sight.

God (GOD) Almighty Creator of the universe; Father. "How great is the love the Father has lavished on us, that we should be called children of God!" See *1 John 3:1*. *God made you special, and he loves you very much.*

godly (GOD-lee) Divine.

gold (GOLD) A valuable metal with a deep yellow color. "These [trials] have come so that your faith–of greater worth than gold . . . may result in praise, glory and honor when Jesus Christ is revealed." See *1 Peter 1:7.*

golden calf (GOAL-den CAFF) A statue that was made by Aaron while Moses was on Mount Sinai when the Israelites got tired of waiting for him.

golden rule (GOAL-den ROOL) One of the best known phrases that people have accepted and taught to others everywhere: "Do to others what you would have them to do to you." See *Matthew 7:12.*

Golgotha (gol-GUH-thuh) This is the hill on which Jesus was crucified. It is an Aramaic word that means "skull."

Goliath (go-LYE-ath) An enormous giant Philistine from Gath whom everyone feared, except for David.

Gomorrah (ga-MORE-ah) A city near Sodom filled with many evil people.

good (GOOD) Pleasant; first-rate; high quality; morally correct. Bob is a very good high jumper and pole vaulter.

good deed An act that is positive and helpful.

goodness (GOOD-nes) The quality or state of being good. "Surely goodness and love will follow me all the days of my life . . ." See *Psalm 23:6.*

Good News (GOOD NOOS) The words the Gospels use to tell us about Jesus. "He said to them, 'Go into all the world and preach the good news to all creation.'" See *Mark 16:15–16.*

Goshen (GOH-shun) A part of Egypt found on the east side of the Nile River, inhabited by the Israelites.

G

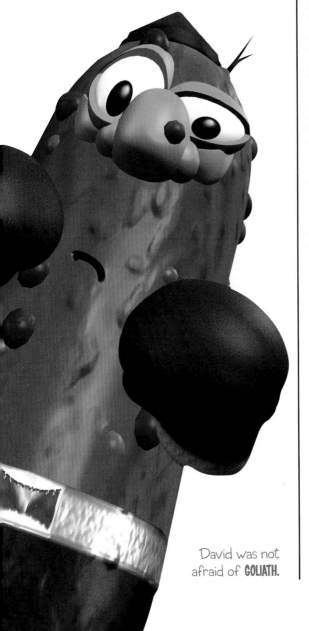

David was not afraid of **GOLIATH.**

gospel (GOS-pul) The truth about the life, death, and resurrection of Jesus Christ.

government (GUV-er-ment) A group of political people who have the power to make and enforce laws for a country.

governor (GUV-er-ner) An elected official who is the head of a state.

grace (GRAYSS) Love, forgiveness, and kindness shown to us, even though we don't deserve it. "It is by grace you have been saved." See *Ephesians 2:5*.

gracious (GRAY-shus) To be well mannered, courteous, and kind.

Grandpa George (GRAN-pah JORJ) A Veggie character in "The Toy That Saved Christmas" whose granddaughter is Annie.

The Grapes of Wrath (GRAYPS of RATH) Very cranky group of grapes that make fun of Junior in "God Wants Me to Forgive Them!?!"

gratitude (grat-i-tood) A feeling of being thankful or glad that someone did something for you. Bob has an attitude of gratitude.

grateful (GRATE-fuhl) Thankful. Bob and Larry are grateful that they can share God's stories with so many people!

GRANDPA GEORGE

grave (GRAYV) A place where a dead person is buried. In Bible times, graves were generally in caves, hewn out in rocks and were closed with big stones.

greed (GREED) Wanting more than you need. Read about greed in *Luke 12:15*. Madame Blueberry showed greed when she had everything she needed but she still wanted more.

grief (GREEF) To be very sad and feel deep pain; to feel heartache over something or someone. Usually grief is felt when someone you love dies.

grow (GROHW) To steadily get bigger; to produce or nurture something. See *1 Corinthians 3:6–7*. The Rumor Weed planted seeds and continued to grow at a rapid pace.

grudge (GRUJ) Deep-seated resentment or ill-will. When you hold onto your grudges, your grudges hold onto you.

grumble (GRUM-bul) To complain quietly, under your breath.

grumpy pants (GRUMP-ee PANTS) A name for someone who is unhappy or cranky. Being greedy makes you a grumpy pants — but a thankful heart is a happy heart.

guarantee (gar-un-TEE) A promise one person makes to another.

guard (GARD) Someone whose job it is to protect someone or something.

guide (GIDE) To lead someone or something. Read about how the Spirit of truth will guide you. See *John 16:13*.

guilt (GILT) A feeling after you know that you've done something wrong. "When he comes, he will convict the world of guilt in regard to sin . . . ." See *John 16:8*. Junior felt guilt after he told a fib.

Habakkuk (ha-BAK-uk) The thirty-fifth book of the Old Testament; a prophet who shared a lot of his complaints and then found hope in God.

Hagar (HAY-gar) Servant of Sarah; mother of Ishmael.

Haggai (HAG-ay-eye) The thirty-seventh book of the Old Testament; a prophet from Jerusalem who spoke greatly of obedience.

hairbrush (HAIR-brush) Tool with a handle and soft bristles used to brush snarls out of hair. One of Larry's favorite songs is "Where is my hairbrush?"

Hallelujah (hal-a-loo-ya) To "Praise the Lord."

Ham (HAMM) Noah's second son.

Haman (HAY-mun) The minister of the Persian emperor who hated the Jews and was hanged for plotting to massacre them.

Hannah (HAN-uh) The mother of Samuel who very much wanted to have a baby for a long time. When she did, she promised that he would serve the Lord.

happy (HAP-ee) Pleased or glad.

The Peach used Larry's **HAIRBRUSH**.

happy heart (HAP-ee HART) A state of being content and feeling good inside. "A happy heart makes the face cheerful . . ." See *Proverbs 15:13*. Madame Blueberry learned that a thankful heart is a happy heart.

harbor (HAR-bur) A port where ships can dock.

harm (HARM) To hurt, damage, or injure something or someone. "Who is going to harm you if you are eager to do good?" See *1 Peter 3:13*.

harmony (HAR-mun-ee) A chord of musical notes that are combined together to form a pleasing sound; the state of being happy together.

harvest (HAR-vest) The time of year when crops are ready to be gathered.

hate (HAYT) To strongly dislike or detest. Read what Luke had to say about hate in *Luke 6:22*. The lesson of Jonah teaches us that we should not hate others, not even those who slap people with fishes, because everyone deserves a second chance.

heal (HEEL) To cure. See *Isaiah 53:5*.

heart (HART) The organ in the body responsible for pumping blood to the rest of the body; an inner part of us from which comes love, compassion, kindness, and affection. "Let love and faithfulness never leave you . . . write them on the tablet of your heart." See *Proverbs 3:3*.

heaven (HEH-vun) The place where people go after death when they believe in God. See *Matthew 6:19–20*.

Hebrews (HEE-broos) What the early Jewish Christians were called; the fourteenth book of letters in the New Testament, written to encourage early Christians to stay strong in their faith.

Hebron (HEE-brahn) A city southwest of Jerusalem where David was anointed king.

heir (AIR) A person who receives something from someone who dies.

hell (HELL) Where the devil lives; a place of eternal punishment.

help (HELP) To assist or lend a hand with. "They also will answer, 'Lord, when did we see you hungry or thirsty or a stranger or needing clothes or sick or in prison, and did not help you?'" See *Matthew 25:44.* God likes it when we are kind and help each other.

hero (HEE-ro) A person admired for his or her achievements and qualities. "I am that HERO!" Larryboy said as he protected the citizens of Bumblyburg.

Herod (HEH-rud) Four different rulers in the New Testament; one of which attempted to kill the infant Jesus by ordering the death of all children under the age of two in Bethlehem.

Hezekiah (hez-eh-KY-uh) King of Judah who sought to abolish idolatry and restore worship to God.

hide (HYD) To conceal something; to place out of sight.

high priest (HY PREEST) A priest with the greatest authority among the Jewish people.

high silk hat (HY SILK HAT) A tall, elegant covering for the head, made of fine material, but does not stand up to the girth of a large squash.

Larryboy is a **HERO**.

hire (HYR) To employ a person to work for you; to pay someone money to do things for you. Rack, Shack, and Benny were hired to work at the chocolate factory.

holy (HOH-lee) Pure; sacred; blessed. "Let him who does right continue to do right; and let him who is holy continue to be holy." See *Revelation 22:11*.

Holy Place (HOH-lee PLAYS) A special place in a tent or temple used to worship God.

Holy Spirit (hoh-lee SPIH-rit) One part of three in the Trinity, along with God and Jesus. We are given the gift of the Holy Spirit to live in us when we decide to believe in Jesus. "But you will receive power when the Holy Spirit comes on you …" See *Acts 1:8*.

honest (AHN-est) To tell the truth.

honor (ON-ur) To show respect for. "Honor your father and mother." See *Luke 18:20*. Honor your parents, because God made them special too.

hope (HOHP) To wish for; to have trust or faith in. "And we rejoice in the hope of the glory of God." See *Romans 5:2*.

Hope (HOHP) The name of the music box angel in "An Easter Carol," who along with Cavis and Millward, must convince Mr. Nezzer that Easter is about more than just candy and eggs.

HOPE

hopeless (HOPE-less) To have no belief in; to feel discouraged.

HORSE

horse (HORS) An animal that was used for transportation, to ride on, and to pull chariots.

Hosanna (hoh-ZAH-nuh) A word used to praise God.

Hosea (hoh-ZEE-ah) The twenty-eighth book of the Old Testament; a prophet of God to Israel.

hospitality (hos-puh-TAL-uh-tee) Kind and welcoming behavior to guests. "Share with God's people who are in need. Practice hospitality." See *Romans 12:13.*

hostility (hos-TIL-ih-tee) A showing of bad feelings toward someone; unfriendliness. There was a sense of hostility between the residents of Flibber-o-Loo and Jibberty-lot.

household (HOWS-hold) The group of people who

The Asparagus **HOUSEHOLD**

live together in a house. "She watches over the affairs of her household and does not eat the bread of idleness." See *Proverbs 31:27.* The Asparagus household consists of Dad, Mom, and Junior Asparagus.

humble (HUM-bul) Not proud, arrogant, or showy. "Be completely humble and gentle; be patient, bearing with one another in love." See *Ephesians 4:2.*

hunger (HUNG-ger) A lack of food; a desire or need for something. "Blessed are those who hunger and thirst for righteousness, for they will be filled." See *Matthew 5:6.* Cheese curls and root beer are a good cure for hunger.

hurt To harm or injure someone physically or emotionally. Bob and Larry don't want to hurt each other's feelings.

hymn (HIM) A praise song to God.

hypocrite (HIP-o-krit) A person who acts a certain way so that others think he is better than they are.

idea (i-DEE-ah) A thought; an inspiration; the spark of imagination. The creation of Bob and Larry was a great, big idea!

idol (I-dul) A false god. "You shall not make for yourself an idol in the form of anything in heaven above or on the earth beneath or in the waters below." See *Exodus 20:4.*

ignore (ig-NOR) To turn away from; to intentionally not take notice.

image (IM-ij) A visual representation of something; picture, impression, or illustration of something. "So God created man in his own image . . ." See *Genesis 1:27.* Pa Grape used a flannelgraph image to teach King George not to be selfish.

H
I

imitate (im-i-TATE) To try to be like someone, to model yourself after another. God wants us to be imitators of Jesus.

Immanuel (i-man-ye-wel) A name for God that means "God with us." See *Matthew 1:23*.

immoral (im-MORE-al) Allowing yourself to be guided by something other than godly principles.

immortality (im-mor-TAL-i-tee) To have eternal life. Jesus gave us life that lasts forever and cannot be taken away.

imperial regiment (im-PEER-ee-ul REH-jih-ment) A group working for the empire.

important (im-POR-tant) Valuable, significant; of great influence. Qwerty shares important messages from the Bible.

imprisoned (im-PRIH-zund) To be put into prison. Despite being imprisoned, Charles Pincher taught Cavis and Millward a little lesson about love in "The Star of Christmas."

incense (IN-sens) A spice that is burned to produce a nice smell. This was sometimes done as a part of worship to God.

inherit (in-HAIR-it) To be left something by someone who leaves or passes away; to come into some kind of gain or position. "Good teacher, what must I do to inherit eternal life?" See *Luke 18:18*.

Charles Pincher was **IMPRISONED.**

inheritance (in-HAIR-ih-tuns) Something passed down

or left to someone else after a person dies or leaves; often done within the family unit.

injury (IN-jur-ee) A wound or pain you get as a result of being hurt, either physically or to your feelings.

injustice (in-JUS-tis) When something is not fair or is wrong. There was an injustice in Dodgeball City in "The Ballad of Little Joe."

inn (IN) A place for weary travelers to rest.

innkeeper (IN-keep-er) The person in charge of an inn.

innocent (IN-oh-sent) Free from guilt or sin.

inspiration (in-spih-RAY-shun) Motivation or encouragement to see, do, or create something. Divine inspiration means "God-breathed." "All Scripture is God-breathed and is useful for teaching, rebuking, correcting and training in righteousness . . ." See *2 Timothy 3:16.*

instruct (in-STRUCT) To explain or teach how to do something. "Listen, my sons, to a father's instruction; pay attention and gain understanding." See *Proverbs 4:1.*

Larry plays his **INSTRUMENT**.

instrument (IN-struh-ment) A tool or devise useful for producing; a piece of equipment often used to make music. Larry the Cucumber can play many instruments. His favorites are the guitar, the tuba, and the accordian.

insult (in-SULT) To use words to hurt someone's feelings.

integrity (in-TEG-rih-tee) Adherence to a policy of truth and honor. Larryboy is a cucumber with integrity and purple plunger ears.

intercede (in-ter-SEED) To plead or step in on someone's behalf. When we pray, the Holy Spirit intercedes for us before God.

interest (IN-trest) Curiosity or concern about something. Bob has an interest in traveling around the world.

interpret (inTUHR-pret) To understand; to explain the meaning of something.

introduce (in-truh-DOOS) To present someone by name to another in order to establish an acquaintance.

invade (in-VAYD) To attack. It was a bad day in Bumblyburg when the Angry Eyebrows invaded and the citizens would not let go of their anger.

invention (in-VEN-shun) Something created or made.

Larry is **INVISIBLE**.

invisible (in-VIS-uh-bul) Something that cannot be seen.

invite (in-VITE) To request formally; to encourage. Barbara Manatee would like Bill to invite her to the ball.

Isaac (I-zak) The son of Abraham and Sarah. He was almost offered as a sacrifice to God. The sacrifice was prevented at the last moment by God, because of Abraham's willingness to obey. See *Genesis 22:1–18.*

Isaiah (i-ZAY-yah) The twenty-third book of the Old Testament; a prophet who lived in Jerusalem giving God's message to his people.

Ishmael (ISH-mah-el) Abraham and Hagar's son. See *Genesis 16.*

This **ISLAND** is surrounded by water.

island (I-lend) A land mass completely surrounded by water. The Island of Perpetual Tickling is a place where people are punished.

Israel (IZ-rah-el) An ancient kingdom of Palestine founded by Saul about 1025 B.C. After 933 it split into the Northern Kingdom, or kingdom of Israel, and the kingdom of Judah to the south.

Israelite (IZ-rah-el-ite) God's people from Israel, which included the 12 tribes of the Jewish nation.

ITALIAN SCALLION

Italian Scallion (ih-TAL-yun SKAL-yun) A Veggie character played by Larry the Cucumber in "Sumo of the Opera." Adopted and raised by scallions, Larry believed himself to be one of them.

JEAN-CLAUDE

jail (JAYL) A building where prisoners are kept for their crimes. Cavis and Millward landed in jail after they stole the Star of Christmas.

Jacob (JAY-cub) Son of Isaac and Rebekah; Joseph's father.

Jacob's well (JAY-cubs WEL) A famous well in Samaria where Jesus tells a woman about living water. See *John 4:4–42* for the story of the woman at the well.

Jairus (JY-rus) A ruler of the synagogue at Capernaum, whose only daughter was restored to life by Jesus. See *Mark 5:22–43*.

James (JAYMS) One of Jesus' twelve disciples. "Jesus called them, and immediately they left the boat and their father and followed him." See *Matthew 4:21–22*.

James (JAYMS) The fifteenth book of letters in the New Testament, believed to be written by James, Jesus' brother.

jammies (JAM-eez) Comfy garments worn at night to sleep in, also great for wearing while you watch VeggieTales.

Japheth (JAF-eth) Noah's youngest son.

jealous (JEL-us) An ugly feeling of wanting what others have; envy. "Because the patriarchs were jealous of Joseph, they sold him as a slave into Egypt. But God was with him and rescued him from all his troubles." See *Acts 7:9–10*.

Jean-Claude(ZHON-KLAWD) One of the Veggie French Peas; likes to wear a beret.

Jehoshaphat (jeh-HOSH-uh-fat) A strong king of Judah who helped to rid Judah of false gods. See *2 Chronicles 17.*

Jehovah (jeh-HOVE-uh) a word used in the Bible for the name of God that means "The Only True God." See *Isaiah 43:10, 11.*

Jeremiah (jer-uh-MY-uh) The twenty-fourth book of the Old Testament; a book of encouragement; a faithful prophet who told the people of Judah not to disobey God.

JERRY GOURD

Jericho (JER-uh-koh) Quite likely one of the oldest cities in the world. Joshua led his people against this city, and God caused the walls to tumble down because the Israelites obeyed him.

Jerry Gourd (JAIR-ee GORD) A Veggie character seen in many VeggieTales episodes; brother of Jimmy Gourd and fellow lover of food.

Jerusalem (jeh-ROO-suh-lem) Also known as the "City of David," this is the place where Jesus and his disciples spent a great deal of time. Jesus was crucified here.

Jesse (JES-ee) King David's father.

Jesus (JEE-zus) God's only Son; born of Mary; he lived a perfect life and was killed on a cross by the Romans to save us from our sins. He rose to life and is back with God in heaven. Jesus is our Savior.

Jethro (JETH-roh) Moses' father-in-law; priest of Midian. See *Exodus 3*.

Jew (JOO) A person from one of the 12 tribes of Jacob.

Jezebel (JEZ-eh-bell) The evil wife of King Ahab. She worshiped the false gods Baal and Asherah. Her bad example led many Israelites to worship false gods.

JIBBERTY-LOT

Jibberty-lot (JIB-ur-tee LOT) A Veggie town where the inhabitants wear pots on their heads; not a good place to get caught wearing a shoe on your head.

jiggle (JIG-ul) To wiggle around. Dr. Jiggle was also dancing Mr. Sly.

JIMMY GOURD

Jimmy Gourd (JIM-ee GORD) A Veggie character in many VeggieTales episodes and the brother of Jerry Gourd; like Jerry, Jimmy enjoys a good snack and the regularly scheduled big yummy meal.

Joab (JOH-ab) King David's nephew and a brave soldier in David's army. See *2 Samuel 10* to learn more about Joab.

Joanna (jo-AN-uh) One of the women that Jesus healed and found the empty tomb where Jesus had been. See *Luke 8:2–3; 24:10.*

Job (JOBE) The eighteenth book of the Old Testament; tells the story of a wealthy man who lost everything important to him and learned that no matter what, God is always in control and loves us very much.

Joel (JO-el) The twenty-ninth book of the Bible; named after the prophet who speaks of judgment and warned the people to obey God.

John (JON) One of Jesus' twelve disciples, and a son of Zebedee. He and his brother, James, were fishermen when Jesus asked them to follow him. The fourth book of the New Testament and final Gospel which tells the story of Jesus' life, death, and resurrection. See *Matthew 4:21–22.*

1 John (FURST JON) The eighteenth book of letters in the New Testament, written by the disciple John to warn of false teachers and to remind people of the promise of salvation.

2 John (SEK-und JON) The nineteenth book of letters in the New Testament, written by the disciple John to warn people of false, traveling teachers.

3 John (THURD JON) The twentieth book of letters in the New Testament, written by the disciple John to support true teachers of the gospel.

John the Baptist (JON the BAP-tist) The son of Elizabeth who preached about Jesus to prepare the way.

join (JOYN) To link or bring things together; to connect to one another. In "An Easter Carol" Mr. Nezzer joined the people of his town at church on Easter Sunday.

J

JONAH

Jonah (JOH-nuh) A prophet whom God asked to go and preach in the city of Nineveh. When Jonah refused, and ran the other way, he was swallowed by a big fish and then spit back out when God gave him a second chance; an Old Testament book written by the prophet, himself, to explain the message of salvation for all people.

Jonathan (JON-uh-thun) The oldest son of King Saul from Israel and friend of David. Read about them in *1 Samuel 20*.

Joppa (JOP-puh) A city where Peter brought Dorcas back to life. See *Acts 9:36–42*.

Jordan River A large river in the country of Palestine. It runs 75 miles from Mount Hermon to the Dead Sea. Jesus was baptized in the Jordan River, near Jericho. See *Mark 1:9*.

Joseph (JOH-sef) Jacob's son who suffered greatly in life and was betrayed by his brothers; he overcame it all and became a great leader.

Joseph of Arimathea (JOH-sef uv air-ih-mah-THEE-uh) A rich man among the Jewish religious court who became a follower of Jesus. He brought Jesus' body down from the cross and buried it in a tomb he provided. See *Matthew 27:57–60*.

Joseph of Nazareth (JOH-sef of NAZ-uh-reth) A carpenter who married Jesus' mother, Mary.

Joshua (JAH-shoo-ah) The sixth book of the Bible; named after Joshua, the man God appointed to be leader of Israel after Moses died.

Josiah (joh-SY-uh) A great and good king of Judah who helped people to understand and obey God's ways. See *2 Kings 21:26* to learn about how Josiah became king when he was eight years old.

journey (JUR-nee) A trip; an expedition; a route that someone travels. Sometimes a journey can be smooth sailing, and other times it's hard, like the journey Jonah took.

joy (JOY) Great happiness; the feeling of love, peace, and delight with God. "Clap your hands, all you nations; shout to God with cries of joy." See *Psalm 47:1*. Larry was so filled with joy that he began to sing a Silly Song.

Judah (JOO-duh) Joseph's brother, son of Jacob; also a kingdom in southern Israel.

Judas Iscariot (JOO-dus i-SKAIR-ee-ot) One of Jesus' twelve disciples who betrayed Jesus by handing him over to the Roman soldiers to be killed.

Jude (JOOD) The twenty-first and final book of letters in the New Testament, written by Jude to early churches in Rome to encourage belief in Jesus Christ.

Judea (joo-DEE-uh) An ancient region of southern Palestine comprising present-day southern Israel and southwest Jordan. In the time of Jesus it was the land of the Jews but ruled by the Roman province of Syria.

judge (JUJ) To evaluate or review; an official person who is in charge of a court. Bob tries not to judge Larry when he pesters him a lot.

J

Judges (JUD-jes) The seventh book of the Bible; this book reminds us that God is firm but also very loving and forgiving.

judgment (JUJ-ment) A final decision of ultimate consequence.

Judgment Day (JUJ-ment DAY) This is the day that Christ will return to judge all people. The people who believe in Jesus will be taken to live with him forever in heaven.

Julius (JOOL-yus) A centurion in charge of Paul as a prisoner, who ultimately let Paul go.

Junior Asparagus (JOON-yur uh-SPAIR-uh-gus) A loveable, young asparagus who is curious, courteous, and . . . green. He attends Veggie Valley Elementary School where he is majoring in aerospace. He lives in Bumblyburg with his mom, Mom Asparagus and his dad, Dad Asparagus.

justice (JUS-tis) Fairness; honesty within rules, the law, or the treatment of one another.

justify (JUS-tih-fy) To prove something is right; to make yourself right with God. "Know that a man is not justified by observing the law, but by faith in Jesus Christ." See *Galatians 2:16*.

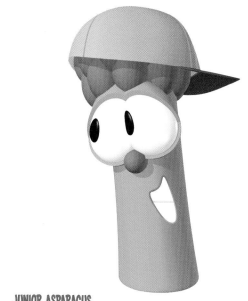

JUNIOR ASPARAGUS

Khalil (kuh-LEEL) Jonah's traveling buddy, he is a

Persian rug salesman who is part worm and part caterpillar, but he is okay with that.

KHALIL

kind (KYND) Caring to others; nice. "Be kind and compassionate to one another, forgiving each other . . ." See *Ephesians 4:32.* Lyle was a kind Viking because he would return the things that the other Vikings would wrongfully take.

king (KING) The ruler of the land.

King Darius (KING DAR-ee-us) King of Persia. See *Ezra 4–6 and Daniel 6* for more about how King Darius ruled in the time of Daniel.

kingdom (KING-dum) The land that is ruled over by a king or queen.

King George (KING JORJ) One of Larry the Cucumber's most challenging roles. Challenging because King George enjoyed taking bubble baths and playing with his rubber ducky. Larry is fairly frightened of rubber duckies and doesn't like bubbles in his bath because they tickle his nose.

K

KING GEORGE

1 Kings (FURST KINGS) The eleventh book of the Old Testament; explains the various rulers of Israel and Judah, including King David.

2 Kings (SEK-und KINGS) The twelfth book of the Old Testament; explains the various rules of Israel and Judah; includes the stories of Elijah and Elisha.

kiss (kis) In early times it would show friendship, love, or respect. Christians would kiss each other on the cheek as a greeting. Jesus was betrayed by a kiss when Judas turned him over to the Roman soldiers.

kneel (NEEL) To rest on one's knees; done as a sign of respect. Although it is hard for a Veggie to kneel, many can be found doing so in the stories they tell from the Bible.

knock (NOK) To rap on something with a gentle fist to call attention.

knowledge (NOL-ij) Accumulated facts that people know to be true; information; facts. "Grow in the grace and knowledge of our Lord and Savior Jesus Christ." See *2 Peter 3:18.* Archibald Asparagus has exhausting knowledge of classical music, Shakespeare, and rare quill pens made from Ostrich feathers in the late 1700's.

Laban (LAY-ban) The father of Leah and Rachel.

labor (LAY-bur) Hard work; An effort toward. "Each will be rewarded according to his own labor." See *1 Corinthians 3:8.*

lake (LAYK) A large body of fresh water and home to many plants and fish. Don't look in a lake for whales, because they live in the ocean.

lamb (LAM) A young sheep, often used by the Jews as a sacrifice to God.

Lamb of God (LAM of GOD) Another name for Jesus because he died as a sacrifice for us to take away our sins. See *John 1:29* where John calls Jesus the Lamb of God.

lame (LAIM) Having a body part and especially an arm or a leg crippled enough so as to be unable to get around without pain or difficulty.

Lamentations (lam-un-TAY-shuns) The twenty-fifth book of the Old Testament that contains five sad poems or songs; believed to be written by the prophet, Jeremiah.

lamp (LAMP) In Bible times, a lamp would look like a small bowl. Olive oil was placed inside, and you would light the wick which would come out of a small spout.

lampstand (LAMP-stand) A tall holder to hold a lamp higher so the light would shine over a larger area.

Lampy (LAMP-ee) A Veggie character that started out as a light source at the end of a pole, but comes to life in the mind of Awful Alvin who really likes to dance with him! *"Dance with me Lampy!"*

language (LANG-gwij) The words, their pronunciation, and the methods of combining them used and understood by a large group of people.

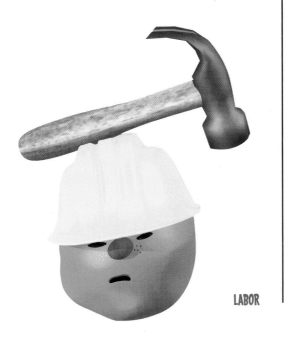

LABOR

Laodicea (lay-ah-deh-SEE-uh) a small town located in what is now Turkey. In Bible times it was an important town where the people were richer than in other towns. John wrote about the church because they were more concerned about making money than serving God.

Larryboy (LAIR-ee-boy) Plunger-headed superhero cuke and alter-ego of Larry the Cucumber; out to save the good folks of Bumblyburg from villains like Awful Alvin. Larryboy is their hero!

LARRYMOBILE

Larrymobile (LAIR-ee-moh-beel) Created by Larryboy's talented and English butler, Alfred, this super-ride is Larryboy's crime-fighting car with super gadgets so it can turn into a plane or a submarine! But can it make waffles?

LARRY THE CUCUMBER

Larry the Cucumber (LAIR-ee thuh KYOO-kum-bur) An extremely silly cucumber who loves to hang out with his pirate friends and do . . . well . . . nothing. Over the years, Larry has portrayed a Viking, Superhero, Cowboy, Pirate, Astronaut and a Sumo Champion.

Last Supper (LAST SUP-er) The last meal Jesus ate with his disciples before he died to celebrate the Passover. See

Matthew 26:17–30 to learn about the Last Supper.

Latin (LAT-in) The language spoken by the Roman people during New Testament times.

LAURA CARROT

Laura Carrot (LOR-ah KARE-ot) A brave and loyal young carrot who loves to help her friends. Laura has two younger brothers, Lenny and Baby Lou, and is Junior Asparagus's best friend.

law (LAW) Rules to live by; the commandments that God gave Moses in the Old Testament. Read about the law of the Lord in *Psalm 19:7.*

Lazarus (LAZ-ah-rus) The brother of Mary and Martha, he was also a close friend to Jesus. When he was sick and died, Jesus brought him back to life. See *John 11:1–44* to learn more about Lazarus's amazing story.

lazy (LAY-zee) Not wanting to work when there are things that need to be done. The Pirates Who Don't Do Anything are quite lazy, yet very funny to watch.

lead (LEED) To be in the very front; to guide or direct others; to be in charge of something.

Leah (LEE-uh) Jacob's wife who had six sons who were fathers of six of the twelve tribes of Israel. See *Genesis 29–30* to learn about this patient and prayerful woman.

leaven (LEV-en) A substance (as yeast or baking powder) that makes dough or batter rise and become light.

L

Lebanon (LEB-uh-nun) A country north of Israel in which Solomon retrieved trees from to build the temple in his palace.

legion (LEE-jun) The chief unit of the Roman army consisting of 3,000 to 6,000 soldiers.

lend (LEND) To let someone borrow something. Bob likes to lend Larry a helping hand—except he doesn't exactly have a hand to lend!

LENNY

Lenny (LEN-ee) Younger brother to Laura Carrot.

leprosy (LEP-ruh-see) A painful skin disease that is highly contagious.

lesson (LES-un) A specific instruction; class or learning session.

Levi (LEE-vi) Joseph's brother, one of Jacob's sons.

Leviathan (lee-VI-ah-than) A sea monster often standing for evil in the Old Testament and Christian literature.

Levite (LEE-vite) A descendant of Levi.

Leviticus (leh-VIT-ih-kus) The third book of the Old Testament about the Levites and what they learned.

liar (LY-ur) Someone that doesn't tell the truth. "If anyone says, 'I love God,' yet hates his brother, he is a liar." See *1 John 4:20.*

light (LYT) The glow or beam from an electrical bulb when a connection is made; an illumination of the mind when an idea sparks.

light bulb (LYT BULB) A light source that screws into a lamp and produces a brightness when turned on that enables you to see.

lily (LIL-ee) A flower that symbolizes new life. There are many varieties of the lily — the Peace Lily, the Tiger Lily, and Snoodle's favorite, the Far Lily.

lima beans (LY-ma beens) A light green vegetable with small white seeds, featured in the VeggieTales theme song.

link (LINGK) A connection with something; to relate to or begin a bond. Don't forget to THINK—LINK—ACT to God's Word before you make a decision.

lion (LY-un) A really big, strong, and mighty cat. Daniel was thrown into a den of lions.

listen (LISS-en) To pay attention to; to use your ears to hear. Junior Asparagus does a good job of listening to his parents.

Little doggies (lit-tul DOH-gees) An American western slang for a calf or baby cow. "Get along little doggies!" Little Joe said to the cattle.

LITTLE JOE

Little Joe (LIT-tul JOH) The Veggie character played by Larry the Cucumber, based on Bible character, Joseph. He endures many hardships at the hands of his brothers and teaches the importance of forgiveness and following God's will.

L

livestock (LIVE-stok) Animals kept or raised; farm animals kept for use and profit.

Living Water (LIV-ing Woter) Jesus explained in *John 4:10* that he was Living Water, and whoever asks for a drink, will receive eternal life.

locust (LOH-kust) A flying insect that eats crops and can be quite a nasty pest.

lonely (LONE-lee) Feeling lost or alone; to be lonesome or wishing that someone else was around. Larry the Cucumber does not like to be lonely, so he's glad he has lots of Veggie friends!

Lord (LORD) Someone who is the master and is in control; another name for Jesus.

Lord's Day (LORDZ dae) The first day of the week. In many countries it is Sunday. Christians meet together on the Lord's Day to rest, worship, and praise God.

Lord's Prayer (LORDZ PRA-r) A name often given to the prayer Jesus taught his disciples as a model for how to pray.

Lord's Supper (LORDZ SUP-ur) The last meal that Jesus shared with his disciples to remind how he was willing to die for us. The bread represents his body and the fruit from the vine reminds us of his blood that was shed for us.

Lot (LOT) Abraham's nephew.

love (LUV) A strong feeling of affection; to care for and be greatly devoted to someone; the way you feel for your family. "And now these three remain: faith, hope and love. But the greatest of these is love." See *1 Corinthians 13:4–8a.*

Lovey (LUV-ee) A veggie character married to the Millionaire marooned in the Veggie Lagoon.

Luke (LOOOK) The third Gospel and book of the New Testament. Luke was one of Jesus' disciples who tells the story of Jesus and focuses on the people Jesus ministered to.

Lydia (LID-ee-uh) A business woman from the city of Thyatira who sold purple cloth and worshiped God. See *Acts 16:13–15* to read how she came to believe in Jesus and what she did afterward.

LYLE THE KINDLY VIKING

Lyle (LY-ul) A Viking played by Junior Asparagus. Lyle is different from all the other Vikings because he is kind to everyone and he doesn't have a horn on his hat.

lyre (LIRE) Small harp held in the hands for playing

Macedonia (ma-sih-DOH-nee-uh) Part of the northern part of Greece where Paul had a vision of a man begging for help.

MADAME BLUEBERRY

Madame Blueberry (MAD-um BLOO-ber-ee) A very proper Blueberry who came to Bumblyburg from France many years ago. She loves to shop at Stuff-Mart for shoes, hats, and small kitchen appliances.

magistrate (maj-i-STRATE) An official who is given authority to uphold laws and to judge over a group of people.

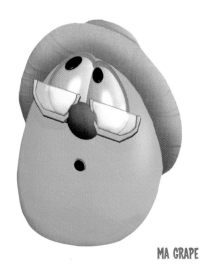

MA GRAPE

Ma Grape (MAH GRAYP) A kindly grape Veggie married to Pa Grape.

maidservant (MADE-servant) A female servant to a wealthy family.

majesty (maj-e-STEE) Royal power, authority, or dignity. Used as a title for a king.

Malachi (MA-lih-ky) The thirty-ninth and last book of the Old Testament; the prophet who encouraged the Jewish people to keep God in their hearts.

manager (MAN-ij-ur) A person who supervises or directs something or someone.

manger (MAIN-jur) A feeding trough for animals; used as a bed for the baby Jesus.

manna (MAN-uh) The food that God sent to the Israelites to eat while they were in the desert. "The Israelites ate manna forty years, until they came to a land that was settled . . ." See *Exodus 16:35.*

manners (MAN-urs) Rules for good behavior.

Mark (MARK) The second Gospel of the New Testament. As a close friend of Peter, Mark wrote about many of the things that Jesus did.

marketplace (MAR-ket-PLAYS) An open place in a town where goods are sold.

marriage (MAIR-ij) The union of a man and woman to become husband and wife.

Martha (MAR-thuh) Friend of Jesus; sister of Mary and Lazarus, who wholeheartedly believed in and loved Jesus.

martyr (MAR-tur) One who suffers for a cause.

Mary (MAIR-ee) Friend of Jesus; sister of Martha and Lazarus who believed in and loved Jesus wholeheartedly.

Mary Magdalene (MAIR-ee MAG-duh-leen) A woman from the town of Magdala who was forgiven by Jesus for things she had done wrong. She loved Jesus with her entire heart and was the first person to see him when he came back to life.

Mary, the Mother of Jesus (MAIR-ee, MUH-thur of JEE-zus). A woman whom God chose to be Jesus' mother and gave birth to God's only Son.

The **MASTER** of Silly Songs!

M

master (MAS-tur) Someone who has authority or control over another; having completely accomplished and become an expert over something. Larry is the master of Silly Songs!

Matthew (MATH-yoo) The first book of the New Testament; Matthew, one of Jesus' 12 disciples, tells the story of Jesus in this first Gospel.

Matthias (mah-THY-us) The disciple that joined the apostles after Judas died. See *Acts 1:26* to see how Matthias was chosen.

Mediterranean Sea (med-ih-tu-RAY-nee-an SEE) A large body of water, surrounded by southern Europe, also referred to as the "Great Sea."

meek (MEEK) Putting up with wrongs patiently and without complaint; humble.

member (MEM-bur) A person who is a part of a group.

Mephibosheth (meh-fib-OH-sheth) The son of Jonathan who was taken care of by King David after Jonathan died.

merchant (MER-chent) Someone who sells something.

mercy (MER-see) Compassion and forgiveness shown to someone after they have done something wrong. In "Jonah, a VeggieTales Movie" there were two things that Junior suddenly saw on the menu: mercy and compassion.

Meshach (ME–shak) Protected in the fiery furnace with Abednego and Shadrach.

messenger (MES-en-jur) Someone who delivers a message or some sort of communication.

Messiah (meh-SY-uh) Another word for Jesus, meaning "the chosen one."

Methuselah (meh-THOO-suh-lah) The oldest man in the Bible who died when he was 969 years old.

Micah (MY-kah) The thirty-third book of the Old Testament; named after the prophet who tries to get the people of Judah to remain faithful to God.

Michael (MY-kul) Archangel or leader of God's angels. Michael works to protect God's people from Satan.

Michal (MY-kul) King Saul's daughter. He used her to try to kill David. She later became David's wife.

Midian (MID-ee-un) One of the sons of Abraham.

mighty (MY-tee) Very powerful and strong—usually of physical nature, but also in will. David wrote about our mighty God in the Psalms. You don't have to be strong to be mighty; you can be mighty in God's eyes by doing what is right.

Larry delivers the **MILK**.

milk (MILK) A white drink that comes from a cow; builds strong bones.

Milk Money Bandit (MILK MUN-ee BAN-dit) A Veggie villain who is out to get milk money.

Millionaire, the (MIL-yun-air) A Veggie character married to Lovey who was marooned in the Veggie Lagoon.

Millward (MIL-werd) A Veggie character who learns about the true meaning of love in "The Star of Christmas."

minister (MIN-ih-ster) Someone who serves God and others.

M

Minnesota Cuke (min-uh-SOH-tah KYOOK) A daring adventure hero played by Larry the Cucumber.

MINNESOTA CUKE

miracle (MIR-uh-cul) An amazing thing that happens with God's help. They were special signs that were used to show God's wonderful and mighty power.

Miriam (MIR-ee-um) The sister of Moses who watched over Moses when he was a baby. See *Exodus 2:1–10* to learn about Miriam's courage in keeping her brother safe.

M

MISS KITTY

Miss Kitty (MIS KIT-ee) The Veggie that got Little Joe in big trouble in the story, "The Ballad of Little Joe."

mistake (mih-STAKE) An error; a slip-up or something done wrong by accident. Larry the Cucumber made a mistake when he thought he needed a hairbrush, because he doesn't have any hair!

Moab (MOH-ab) The land where Ruth lived. It was named for Lot's son.

Moby Blaster (MOH-bee BLAST-er) A really cool Veggie video game from the movie, "Jonah, a VeggieTales Movie."

money (MUN-ee) Coin or special paper used to pay for things.

money changers (MUN-ee CHANJ-ers) People who exchanged one kind of money for another to assist others in paying for something. They were often set up in the temple courtyards which prevented some of the Jewish people from praying or worshiping God.

monster (MON-ster) A scary creature that makes

you afraid. God is bigger than the boogeyman. He's bigger than Godzilla or the monsters on TV!

Mordecai (MOR-dih-ky) Raised Esther and allowed himself to be used by God in powerful ways to help save the Jewish people when Haman was trying to kill them. See *Esther 2–6.*

Moses (MOH-zes) Great chosen leader by God who led God's people out of Egypt; received the Ten Commandments; and wrote the first five books of the Bible.

Most Holy Place A special room in the meeting tent the ark of the covenant was kept. Only the high priest could enter this room.

Mount Ginchez (MOUNT GIN-chez) A mountain near Snoodleburg, home to the red-snootered finches.

Mount of Olives (MOUNT of OL-ihvs) A ridge east of Jerusalem filled with olive trees. The Garden of Gethsemane is located here, where Jesus prayed before being arrested by the Romans.

Mount Sinai (MOUNT SYE-nye) The holy mountain where God spoke to Moses and gave him the Ten Commandments. See *Exodus 19:20–25.*

mourn (MORN) To grieve; to feel sad after something or someone has died.

M

MR. LUNT

Mr. Lunt (MIS-ter LUNT) A funny Veggie gourd with a slight Spanish accent who works with Mr. Nezzer.

MR. MCPOTIPHER

Mr. McPotipher (MIS-ter mac-POT-ih-fur) The Veggie that gave Little Joe a job.

Mr. Sly (MIS-ter SLY) The alter ego of Dr. Jiggle. Although you can't tell from appearances, Mr. Sly is a direct descendant of a disco dancer.

Mr. Twisty (MIS-ter TWIST-ee) The Veggie who played the king of Nineveh

and created the most delicious cheese curls you've ever tasted!

murder (MUR-der) To kill someone.

myrrh (MUR) A special tree gum liquid used as perfume and in healing. See *Matthew 2:11.*

mystery (MIS-tu-ree) Something that has not been or cannot be explained.

MR. SLY

Naaman (NAY-uh-mun) A leader of the Aramean army who was healed of leprosy by Elisha.

Naomi (nay-OH-mee) The mother-in-law of Ruth who stayed with her daughter-in-law and helped her to meet her next husband, Boaz.

nard (n-ARE-d) An expensive perfume imported from India.

Nathan (NAY-thun) A prophet who told David that his son, Solomon, was going to build the Temple. He was responsible for Solomon's place as king after David's reign.

Nathanael (nuh-THAN-yul) One of Jesus' twelve disciples.

nation (NAY-shun) A group of people who live in the same area and are under the same rule.

nature (NA-chur) Natural scenery that God made; the world; the character of a person.

naughty (NAW-tee) Doing something wrong and breaking the rules. It is naughty to kick a soccer ball in most church worship areas.

Nazarene (NAZ-uh-reen) A person from the town of Nazareth.

Nazareth (NAZ-uh-reth) A town in the region of Galilee where Jesus lived.

near (NEAR) Close to. "But as for me, it is good to be near God." See *Psalm 73:28*.

Nebuchadnezar (neb-uh-kad-NEZ-ur) King of Babylon who destroyed Jerusalem.

need (NEED) To lack something that is necessary. Sometimes we confuse things that we want with what we need, like a Buzz-Saw Louie doll.

N

Nehemiah (nee-uh-MY-uh) The sixteenth book of the Old Testament; he was a good and strong leader who helped the Jews rebuild the walls of Jerusalem.

neighbor (NAY-bur) A fellow friend; someone you live near. "Love your neighbor as yourself." See *Matthew 19:19*. In the VeggieTales story, "Are You My Neighbor?" we learn how to love others, even though they look or act differently.

N

New Testament (NU TEST-uh-ment) The books of the Bible that begin with the coming of Jesus and then relate to his life, death, and resurrection. The first four books are the Gospels. The next twenty-one books are letters written to help the early churches learn to follow in God's way and trust Jesus as their Savior. The last book is Revelation, which is a vision given to John about the future.

Nicodemus (nik-uh-DEE-mus) He was a Jewish ruler who came to believe in Jesus.

Snoodles love **NOODLES**.

Nile River (NYL RIV-er) A river that flows in Egypt into the Mediterranean Sea. It was turned to blood to threaten and punish the Egyptians who would not let the Hebrews go free.

Nineveh (NIN-uh-vuh) A town in which many people did not believe in God and did wrong.

Noah (NOH-uh) The man God trusted to build an ark that would hold his family and two of each kind of animal so he could flood the earth and rid it of all the people who had sinned. See *Genesis 6* for the story of Noah and the ark.

noodle (NOO-dul) A ribbon-shaped pasta that Snoodles enjoy eating with pancakes.

noteworthy (NOTE wer-the) Worthy of note; remarkable; important.

nourish (NUR-ish) To feed or nurture.

Numbers (NUM-burs) The fourth book of the Old Testament; named after the two countings of the Israelites while they were wandering in the desert, waiting to enter the Promised Land.

oath (OHTH) A pledge taken; a promise made. "Do not break your oath, but keep the oaths you have made to the Lord." See *Matthew 5:33.* The boy made an oath to his mother that he would eat all of his oatmeal after he put sardines in it.

Obadiah (oh-buh-DY-yuh) The thirty-first book of the Old Testament; named after the prophet who reminds the people that God is truly in control and will punish those who do not follow his ways.

obedience (oh-BEE-dee-ence) The act of listening and doing what you are told. "And this is love: that we walk in obedience to his commands." See *2 John 1:6.*

obey (oh-BAY) To do what you are supposed to do. Rack, Shack, and Benny chose to obey God and did not bow down to the bunny.

observe (ob-ZURV) To watch or look at; to study. "Observe the commands of the Lord your God, walking in his ways and revering him." See *Deuteronomy 8:6.*

N
O

obtain (ob-TAIN) To get something; to acquire or achieve.

obvious (OB-vee-us) Plain to see or understand; clear. It is obvious that Bob and Larry are great friends.

occasion (oh-KAY-zhun) A special time for something to take place; a circumstance; a chance occurrence. In the VeggieTales theme song, all the Veggies have an occasion to welcome you to the show.

occupation (ahk-yoo-PAY-shun) A job; a profession; a career.

occupy (AHK-yoo-py) To live in; to fill a space; to have something that takes up your time. Whenever Larry is looking for something to do, he writes a Silliy Song to occupy his time.

offend (uh-FEND) To hurt someone's feelings; to insult someone. See *John 6:61* where Jesus asks, "Does this offend you?" If you do not eat the squid-jelly donuts and pie that Grandma made, you may offend her.

offer (AW- fur-ur) To make a suggestion; to present something to another; to intentionally give something to someone. "Offer your bodies as living sacrifices, holy and pleasing to God." See *Romans 12:1.* Larry offered to teach Bob how to sing and dance, but Bob felt he already knew how.

offering (AW-fer-ing) A gift or donation to another.

official (oh-FISH-ul) Someone who holds a position or office. Jimmy and Jerry Gourd offered to be the official taste testers at the upcoming food fair, but there wasn't enough food.

offspring (AWF-spring) The "children" of a person, plant, or animal.

oil (OYL) A substance used in Bible times for food preparation, fuel, and healing. It was also utilized for anointing someone for a special position.

Okie Dokie Corral (OH-kee DOH-kee kor-AL) The place where Little Joe and his family live.

OLAF

Olaf (OH-lahf) A Veggie Viking of the sea played by Mr. Nezzer in "Lyle the Kindly Viking."

Old Testament (OLD TEST-uh-ment) The first 39 books of the Bible, representing the time before Christ was born. It starts with God's creation of all that is good and includes many of God's teachings as he prepared his people for the coming of his Son. It includes the books of law, history, poetry, and prophecy.

omega (oh-MAY-guh) The last one; the end of all things. See *Revelation 21:6.*

Onesimus (oh-NES-ih-mus) A slave who, after robbing his master Philemon at Colosse, fled to Rome. There he was converted by the apostle Paul, who sent him back to his master with the letter which bears his name asking Philemon to release Onesimus.

organize (OR-gan-ize) To put together in an orderly way. Alfred was good at organizing Larryboy's special gadgets.

orphan (OR-fun) A young person who is without parents or another person willing to care and love him or her. See *James 1:27* to find out how the Bible says we should take care of orphans.

OTTAR

Ottar (OH-tur) A Veggie Viking of the sea played by Bob the Tomato.

ought (AWT) Something that should be.

oui (WEE) The word for "yes" in the French language, said by the French Peas.

outcome (OUT-come) How something ends. The outcome of the wrestling match between the Italian Scallion and Apollo Gourd was a tie.

outlet (OUT-let) The place where something is let out; an electrical channel used to make a connection. The power outlet was used to connect electricity to the light, and suddenly, Lampy lit up!

outstretch (out-STRECH) To reach out, extend.

oven (UV-en) A place for baking food or heating metal. In Bible times the ovens were made out of clay. They were shaped like large overturned barrels, and the fire was placed at the bottom.

overboard (OH-vur bord) The word used to describe someone who falls out of a boat. Jonah was not thrown overboard; he was forced to walk off the plank.

overcome (oh-vur-KUM) To defeat something; to

survive a challenge. Jesus said, "But take heart! I have overcome the world." See *John 16:33.*

overflow (O-ver-FLO) To cover with; to flow over the brim or top of; to fill a space up and spread beyond its limits.

owe (OH) To have the responsibility to pay back something. "Give everyone what you owe him . . ." See *Romans 13:7.*

ox (äks) A large, domestic cattle. It is kept for milk, draft, and meat. The female is called a cow and the male a bull.

pagan (PAY-gun) A person who has no faith in God.

Pa Grape (PAH GRAYP) A wise, old veggie grape.

pain (PAYN) What you feel when something hurts, either physically or emotionally. See *Revelation 21:4* to learn about how God promises there will be no more pain in heaven.

palace (PAL-is) A large place where an important leader may live.

palm tree (PAHM-tree) A tropical tree.

Palmy (PAHM-ee) A Veggie tree on the beach who sang about forgiveness. When Palmy went on vacation to Hawaii, he was the only singing palm tree on the island!

PA GRAPE

papyrus (puh-PY-rus) A plant used to make paper when it is pressed flat.

parable (PAIR-uh-bul) A story with an important lesson. "Jesus spoke all these things to the crowd in parables; he did not say anything to them without using a parable." See *Matthew 13:34.* The parable of the Good Samaritan teaches that we should love our neighbor and treat others like we would want to be treated.

paradise (PAIR-uh-dice) Heaven; a beautiful, perfect place.

paralyzed (PAIR-uh-lized) Physically unable to move.

parchment (PARCH-ment) An animal skin, dried out, and used to write on.

pardon (PAR-dun) To grant forgiveness to.

parents (PAIR-ents) The people who give birth to and raise children in a family. "Children, obey your parents in the Lord, for this is right." See *Ephesians 6:1.*

passion (PASH-un) A very strong feeling for an object or purpose.

Passover (PAS-oh-ver) A Jewish holiday celebrating the Hebrew's freedom from slavery in Egypt.

past (PAST) What has already been. Mr. Nezzer visits Easter past with the help of Hope in "An Easter Carol."

pastor (PAST-ur) A minister who serves in a church or other Christian organization.

pasture (PAS-chur) An area of land kept for animals to graze on.

path (PATH) A prepared way to get somewhere. "Teach me your way, O LORD; lead me in a straight path. . ." See *Psalm 27:11.*

patience (PAY-shuns) The quality or state of being patient.

patient (PAY-shunt) Someone under the care of a doctor; calm and not complaining about having to wait for something. Larry was the patient from Flibber-o-loo who was helped by his new friend from Jibberty-lot.

Paul (PAWL) An apostle of Jesus; worked hard to spread the good news about Jesus.

peace (PEES) A state of calm. "And the peace of God, which transcends all understanding, will guard your hearts and your minds in Christ Jesus." See *Philippians 4:7.*

peacemaker (PEES-maykur) Someone who actively tries to resolve conflicts. "Blessed are the peacemakers, for they will be called sons of God." See *Matthew 5:9.*

pearl (PERL) A dense, smooth, shiny body that is considered a gem and is formed in a shell. Jesus told a parable about a pearl of great value in *Matthew 13:45.*

PENGUIN

P

penguin (PEN-gwin) A fun arctic animal that works in the toy factory. In "The Toy That Saved Christmas," the penguins worked as security guards in the toy factory.

Pentateuch (PENT-uh-took) The name of the first five books of the Old Testament.

Pentecost (PENT-ih-cost) The day the Holy Spirit came upon the disciples.

PERCY

Percy (PUR-see) A Veggie pea who's good friends with Junior and Laura.

perfect (PUR-fect) Having no failures or problems. "As for God, his way is perfect; the word of the Lord is flawless." See *Psalm 18:30.*

perform (per-FORM) To act, sing, or dance in front of an audience. Twippo performs for the Veggies in "Jonah, a VeggieTale Movie."

perfume (pur-FYOOM) Liquid made from flowers, worn to smell good.

persecute (PUR-suh-kyoot) To harm or tease because of a belief. "Rejoice and be glad, because great is your reward in heaven, for in the same way they persecuted the prophets who were before you." See *Matthew 5:12.*

persevere (pur-suh-VEER) To hang in there when something gets hard. "You need to persevere so that when you have done the will of God, you will receive what he has promised." See *Hebrews 10:36.* In order to move Madame Blueberry's piano up the flight of stairs, her friends had to persevere.

Persia (PUR-zhuh) A former country in the Middle East; Iran today.

Peter (PEE-tur) Jesus' disciple who walked on water to Jesus .

1 Peter (FURST PEE-tur) The sixteenth book of letters in the New Testament, written by Peter which included much suffering, hope, and joy.

2 Peter (SEK-und PEE-tur) The seventeenth book of letters in the New Testament, written by Peter to guide people away from false teachings.

petition (puh-TISH-un) A request. "So I turned to the Lord God and pleaded with him in prayer and petition ..." See *Daniel 9:3*.

pew (PEEOO) A bench that people, or Veggies, sit on in church. When Mr. Nezzer was a young boy, he sat in the first pew at St. Bart's church with his grandma in "An Easter Carol."

Pharisee (FAIR-uh-see) Member of the Jewish sect who is very strict about their rules and laws.

Pharaoh (FAIR-oh) Ruler of Egypt.

Philemon (fih-LEE-mun) The thirteenth book of letters in the New Testament where Paul encourages Philemon, a slave owner, to see his slaves as equals.

Philip (FIL-up) One of Jesus' 12 disciples.

Philippe (fih-LEEP) A Veggie French Pea related to Jean Claude and Percy.

Philippians (fih-LIP-ee-uns) The sixth book of letters in the New Testament, written by Paul while he was imprisoned for the first time; speaks of joy.

Philistines (FIL-uh-steens) Battled the Israelites.

pickle (PIK-ul) A vegetable that Larry is often mistaken for; a problem. Larry is constantly telling people, "I'm not a pickle; I'm a cucumber."

I'm not a **PICKLE.**

P

Pontius Pilate (PAHN-chus PY-lut) The Roman leader who ordered Jesus to be crucified.

plagues (PLAYGZ) An outbreak of something unpleasant; a disease; a curse. See *Exodus 9:13–14*.

plan (PLAN) To identify the steps to accomplish something; to map something out; to create an arrangement; to prepare. "'For I know the plans I have for you,' declares the Lord, 'plans to prosper you and not to harm you, plans to give you hope and a future.'" See *Jeremiah 29:11*.

plank (PLANGK) A wooden board. In the movie, "Jonah, a VeggieTales Movie," Jonah had to walk the plank.

please (PLEEZ) To give satisfaction to; a good manner when you are asking for something.

plentiful (PLEN-ti-ful) Having a lot of. "He told them,

'The harvest is plentiful, but the workers are few.'" See *Luke 10:2*.

plug (PLUG) To connect one thing to another using a power source.

poem (PO-um) A written verse that may or may not rhyme.

polite (puh-LYTE) To have good manners.

Larry plays a **POLKA.**

polka (POLE-kuh) A fun dance originating from Bohemia. Larry teaches about homophones in The Schoolhouse Polka in "Sumo of the Opera."

poor (PORE) Not having much money; to be unfortunate; to be weak. "Blessed are you who are poor, for yours is the kingdom of God." See *Luke 6:20.*

possess (poh-ZES) To own.

possession (poh-ZEH-shun) Something that you own.

POT

pot (POT) A tool used to cook things in; can be used as a hat. The Veggies of Jibberty-lot wear pots on their heads in "Are You My Neighbor?"

Potiphar (POT-uh-far) Bought Joseph from the Midianites; Pharoah's official, the captain of the guard.

potter (POT-ur) Someone who makes things from clay. "We are the clay, you are the potter; we are all the work of your hand." See *Isaiah 64:8.*

poverty (POV-ur-tee) Living in very poor conditions.

power (POW-er) Authority; the ability to take charge, be in control, and make things happen. Strength, might, and energy. Read *Ephesians 1:18–19* to hear about God's great power.

powerful (POW-er-ful) Having a lot of influence.

practice (PRAK-tis) To do something over and over in order to improve.

P

praise (PRAYZ) To tell someone positive things; to give glory. "I will praise you, O LORD, with all my heart; I will tell of all your wonders." See *Psalm 9:1*.

pray (PRAY) To spend time thoughtfully in conversation with God. Jonah would always pray to God at night before he went to bed.

prayer (PRAIR) The requests, praises, and thanks brought to God in conversation. "Therefore I tell you, whatever you ask for in prayer, believe that you have received it, and it will be yours." See *Mark 11:24*.

preach (PREECH) To tell people the Good News of Jesus, God, and the Holy Spirit.

precious (PREH-shus) Delicate; special to someone. A name for a very powerful bean if you happen to find one.

prepare (prih-PAIR) To get ready. "And if I go and prepare a place for you, I will come back and take you to be with me . . . " See *John 14:3*.

presence (PREZ-ens) The fact or state of being present.

present (PREZ-ent) The current time; the here and now. A gift.

pretend (prih-TEND) To act as if something is really happening when it isn't. Phil Winkelstein pretends to be Frankencelery in "Where's God When I'm S-Scared!?!"

price (PRYS) The cost of something. "You are not your own; you were bought at a price." See *1 Corinthians 6:19–20*.

Pricilla (Pri-SIL-uh) A Jewish Christian from Rome who traveled with Paul. She and her husband, Aquila, worked as tentmakers.

priest (PREEST) An authorized person who performs sacred, religious rites.

prince (PRINS) The son of a king.

PRINCESS PETUNIA

Princess Petunia (PRIN-ses peh-TOON-ya) A pretty young petunia Veggie character.

priority (pry-OR-ih-tee) Something of greater importance than other things.

prison (PRIZ-un) The place where prisoners are kept.

prisoner (PRIZ-un-ur) Someone who has broken the law; a captive. "As a prisoner for the Lord, then, I urge you to live a life worthy of the calling you have received." See *Ephesians 4:1*. Little Joe was kept as a prisoner in the jail at Dodgeball City.

problem (PROB-lem) A question or situation that needs an answer.

proclaim (proh-KLAYM) To tell with energy.

prodigal (PROD-ih-gul) Wasteful; reckless. See *Luke 15:11–32* for the story of the prodigal son.

produce (PRUH-doos) To make something. The chocolate factory workers produce millions of chocolates every year.

productivity (proh-duk-TIV-it-tee) Getting work done at a good rate.

Professor (proh-FESS-ur) A Veggie inventor marooned at the Veggie Lagoon.

P

progress (PRAH-gres) Moving forward.

promise (PRAH-mis) A pledge to do something; an assurance; to swear or guarantee you will do something; to take an oath. Read about God's promise to Abraham in *Hebrews 6:13–15*.

Josh was going to the **PROMISED LAND.**

Promised Land (PRAH-mist LAND) The land God promised to Abraham and his people. Joshua was on his way to the Promised Land when he encountered the Big Wall at Jericho.

property (PRAH-pur-tee) The things you have; things that belong to you; land. "And if you have not been trustworthy with someone else's property, who will give you property of your own?" See *Luke 16:12*.

prophesy (PROF-uh-see) To predict; to foretell the future.

prophet (PROF-it) A person God reveals something to and asks to share it with others. Jonah was a prophet.

prosper (PROS-per) To succeed; to thrive, to flourish.

protect (proh-TEKT) To guard something from being damaged. "I will protect him, for he acknowledges my name." See *Psalm 91:14*.

proud (PROUD) Arrogant and conceited; pleased with yourself; to be full of pride. "God opposes the proud but gives grace to the humble." See *1 Peter 5:5*. The Flibbians were quite proud of the shoes they wore on their heads.

PROUD of their shoes

Proverbs (PRAH-verbs) The twentieth book of the Old Testament; encourages us to gain wisdom and steer clear of trouble.

provision (pro-VIZH-un) Something done beforehand, preparation; a stock of materials or supplies.

Psalms (SAHMS) The nineteenth book of the Old Testament; a comforting book of prayers and praise to God.

Puggslyville (PUGS-lee-vil) Veggie town where children learn the true meaning of Christmas.

P

punish (PUN-ish) To inflict a penalty when you break a rule. Read about how the Lord loves and punishes his people in *Hebrews 12:5–6*.

pure (PYOUR) Kept apart and untainted by other things. "Finally, brothers, whatever is true, whatever is noble, whatever is right, whatever is pure . . . think about such things." See *Philippians 4:8*.

purify (PYOOR-ih-fy) To make clean.

purpose (PUR-pus) A reason for; an intention; to have determination for something. See *2 Thessalonians 1:11–12.*

quality (KWAL-ih-tee) A characteristic of excellence; a specific feature.

quantity (KWAN-tih-tee) The number of something.

quarrel (KWOR-ul) A verbal argument. "He who loves a quarrel loves sin." See *Proverbs 17:19.*

queen (KWEEN) The female ruler of a land. Esther became a queen when she married King Xerxes.

quest (KWEST) An exciting journey with a purpose.

quibble (KWIB-ul) To argue. Sometimes Bob and Larry quibble when Larry is working around the set with his power tools.

quiver (KWIH-vur) A bag that is used to hold arrows. In *Isaiah 49:2*, the Bible says that God is like a quiver. God keeps us safe like the quiver keeps the arrows safe.

QWERTY

Qwerty (KWERT-ee) The Veggie computer that sits on the kitchen countertop and produces Bible verses that help teach kids what God wants them to learn.

rabbi (RAB-eye) A master teacher. A title of dignity given by the Jews to their distinguished teachers. It is sometimes applied to Christ.

Rachel (RAY-chul) Jacob's wife, sister of Leah, mother of Joseph and Benjamin.

RACK

Rack (RAK) Worked in Mr. Nezzer's chocolate factory with his brothers, Shack and Benny; or something you can hang your hat on.

rage (RAYJ) Extreme anger; fuming temper; seething wrath. "Get rid of all bitterness, rage and anger, brawling and slander, along with every form of malice." See *Ephesians 4:31.*

Rahab (RAY-hab) A faithful woman who helped Joshua by hiding his spies.

rainbow (RAIN-boh) A colorful arch seen in the sky when it's raining and the sun is out; a symbol of God's promise to not flood the earth again.

ranch (RANCH) A type of home with a farm used for raising various animals. Little Joe and his family live on a ranch in "The Ballad of Little Joe."

R

ransom (RAN-sum) A price paid in exchange for something. "Christ Jesus, who gave himself as a ransom for all men . . ." See *1 Timothy 2:5–6.*

raven (RAY-ven) A black bird.

ravine (rah-VEEN) A small, deep valley usually formed from running water.

read (REED) To interpret letters into words and understand what they say.

ready (RED-ee) Prepared for an activity. "So you also must be ready, because the Son of Man will come at an hour when you do not expect him." See *Matthew 24:44*.

reap (REEP) To collect and obtain a harvest.

reason (REE-zun) An explanation; a motive; a rationale. To give an explanation. Something that makes good sense. Junior learned the reason for not watching scary movies before bed is that it may make him too afraid to go to sleep.

reassure (rE-a-shuer) to be sure or certain, not to doubt or fear.

Rebekah (ruh-BEK-uh) Isaac's wife.

rebel (rih-BEL) To act out; disobey.

rebuke (rih-BYOOK) To reprimand; to tell someone you don't approve.

receive (rih-SEEV) To get something from someone.

reckon (REK-un) To consider something. Little Joe's family reckoned they made a mistake in selling their brother.

recognize (REK-ug-nize) To acknowledge; to be familiar with; to appreciate.

reconcile (rek-un-sile) To make amends; to settle a problem. "All this is from God, who reconciled us to himself through Christ and gave us the ministry of reconciliation . . ." See *2 Corinthians 5:18*.

redeem (rih-DEEM) To compensate; to trade for something; to be released from.

redeemer (rih-DEEM-ur) A savior; a rescuer. "Our Redeemer

—the LORD Almighty is his name . . ." See *Isaiah 47:4.*

Red Sea (RED SEE) A place where the Israelites headed when they left Egypt. With the help of God, Moses parted it to allow the Israelites to pass through so they could escape from the Egyptian army.

red-snootered finches (red-snoot-urd FINCHS) A bird native to Snoodleburg residing in Mount Ginches.

reform (rih-FORM) To improve or change something; to transform.

reign (RAIN) To have absolute power or sovereignty. "And [Jesus] will reign for ever and ever." See *Revelation 11:15.*

reject (rih-JEKT) To refuse; to turn away.

rejoice (rih-JOYS) To celebrate and express joy. "Rejoice in the Lord always. I will say it again: Rejoice!" See *Philippians 4:4.*

Junior's and his Dad's **RELATIONSHIP**

relationship (rih-LAY-shun-ship) An association or friendship with another; a special connection with someone. The relationship between Junior and his dad is very special!

relief (rih-LEEF) To take away something painful; to assist.

renew (ri-NOO) To make or become new, fresh, or strong again.

R

remain (rih-MAYN) To stay put; to linger; to continue. "Remain in me, and I will remain in you." See *John 15:4.*

remember (rih-MEM-bur) To regain the memory of something; to retain information; to recall. "I thank my God every time I remember you." See *Philippians 1:3.*

remnant (REM-nent) Something that remains or is left over.

repay (rih-PAY) To pay back.

repent (rih-PENT) To change one's life for the better; for forgiveness and to feel remorse. "The kingdom of God is near. Repent and believe . . ." See *Mark 1:15.*

reply (rih-PLY) To answer or respond.

R

request (rih-KWEST) To ask for something; to make an appeal. Bob made a request that Larry clean up the dust bunnies under his bed.

requirement (rih-KWYR-ment) An obligation; a necessity.

Hope they **RESCUE** Larry.

rescue (RES-kyoo) To save; to free or release. While stranded at the Veggie Lagoon, Bob and Larry hoped to be rescued.

respect (rih-SPEKT) To show honor, esteem; to admire. "Now we ask you, brothers, to respect those who work hard among you…" See *1 Thessalonians 5:12.*

responsibility (rih-spon-sih-BIL-ih-tee) Being accountable for; a duty toward something; dependablity. Jimmy and Jerry took responsibility for eating Bob's collection of dinner mints.

restore (rih-STOR) To put something in its original state.

resurrection (rez-uh-REK-shun) To rise again. "Jesus said to her, 'I am the resurrection and the life.'" See *John 11:25.*

Reuben (ROO-ben) Joseph's brother; asked his brothers to spare Joseph; wanted to rescue Joseph.

Revelation (rev-uh-LAY-shun) The final book of the New Testament; a book of hope in Christ and good over evil.

revenge (rih-VENJ) A retribution taken after a wrong was done; a payback.

Reverend Gilbert (REV-ur-und GIL-burt) A Veggie character in "An Easter Carol."

REVEREND GILBERT

S

reward (rih-WARD) A prize for doing something well; a payment for something well done; a bonus or gift. "You will receive an inheritance from the Lord as a reward." See *Colossians 3:24.*

Rhoda (ROH-duh) A servant girl in the house of Mary, the mother of John, also named Mark. See *Acts 12.*

riches (RICH-ez) The money, treasures, or resources one has.

right (RYT) Correct, true, accurate. Little Joe's brothers did the right thing when they asked him for forgiveness.

righteous (RY-chus) Virtuous; morally correct; just; blameless. "He saved us, not because of righteous things we had done, but because of his mercy." See *Titus 3:5.*

rise (RYZ) To raise up; to climb or ascend.

risk (RISK) To take a chance.

Romans (ROH-muns) Citizens of Rome; the first book of letters in the New Testament written by Paul sharing the wonder of God's grace.

Rome (RO-m) The current capital of Italy and the capital city of the Roman Empire at the time of Christ. It is said to have been founded in 753 B.C. Paul's book of Romans was to the Christians who lived in Rome.

root beer (ROOT beer) A carbonated, quite foamy, and deliciously yummy drink that The Pirates Who Don't Do Anything love to drink. The Pirates Who Don't Do Anything drink root beer whenever they can—so maybe they do like to do something after all!

Rootin' Tootin' Pizza Place (ROOT-in TOOT-in PEET-zuh plays) Where Little Joe and Miss Kitty worked for Mr. McPotiphar in "The Ballad of Little Joe."

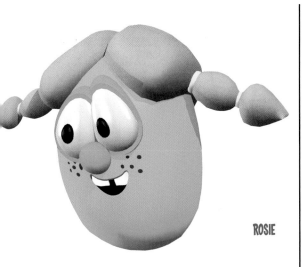

ROSIE

Rosie (ROHZ-ee) A grape Veggie character, sister to Tom grape.

rubber ducky (RUB-er DUK-ee) A fun, yellow toy that Larry plays with in the bathtub. You might have one too!

ruin (ROO-in) To destroy; to damage or wreck.

rule (ROOL) A law; a regulation. To govern or administrate; to have power over someone or something. "Let the peace of Christ rule in your hearts . . ." See *Colossians 3:15.*

ruler (ROOL-er) Someone who reigns/rules; a leader who creates laws.

Ruth (ROOTH) The eighth book of the Old Testament; this book tells the story of Ruth and her family and focuses on faith and love.

Sabbath (SAB-uth) A Jewish word meaning, "to rest"; this is referred to as the seventh day of creation, when God rested. It is also referred to in God's Ten Commandments.

sackcloth (SAK-cloth) Clothing worn, made from goat's hair, during a period of sadness and grief.

sacred (SAY-kred) Holy, set apart because it's for God. "God's temple is sacred, and you are that temple." See *1 Corinthians 3:17.* Rack, Shack, and Benny would not worship the chocolate bunny, because they knew it was not sacred.

R
S

sacrifice (SAK-rih-fice) To give something up.

SAD

sad (SAD) A feeling of misery or gloom. Junior Asparagus was sad that the Peas were calling him a bean boy; he's an asparagus and proud of it!

saddlebags (SAD-ul-bags) A pouch that lays over the saddle of a horse to carry things. Little Joe's brothers returned home with their saddlebags full of food.

Sadducees (SAD-you-seez) A Jewish religious group. They were important and wealthy men who believed that only the first five books of the Old Testament were true. They did not believe in angels or Christ's resurrection.

safe (SAYF) Protected from harm; secure; reliable or dependable. An indestructible place to put money. "Keep me safe, O God, for in you I take refuge." See *Psalm 16:1.* Josh and the other Veggies were not safe from the slushies that were tossed from the French Peas on the wall of Jericho.

saint (sAnt) A holy and godly person; one who is declared to be worthy of special honor. Christians are also called "saints." See *Ephesians 1:1.*

Salome (SAL-oh-may) The wife of Zebedee; she was at Jesus' death and also went to Jesus' tomb and saw him after he came back to life.

salt (SALT) A seasoning to add flavor; a food preservative. The ocean water at Veggie Lagoon was full of salt.

S

salvation (sal-VAY-shun) Deliverance; a rescue from. Jesus gives us salvation through his death by rescuing us from sin. "You are receiving the goal of your faith, the salvation of your souls." See *1 Peter 1:9.*

Samaria (suh-MAIR-ee-uh) Between Galilee and Judea, this was a strong early church town where the people who lived there were only part Jewish.

Samaritan (suh-MAIR-uh-tun) A person from Samaria.

Samson (SAM-sun) A judge from Israel; he had special strength that helped the Israelites fight the Philistines.

Samuel (SAM-yoo-ul) A prophet who anointed David to replace Saul as king.

1 Samuel (FURST SAM-yoo-ul) The ninth book of the Old Testament; recalls the lives of Samuel, Saul, and much of David.

2 Samuel (SEK-und SAM-yoo-ul) The tenth book of the Old Testament; tells of David's reign over Israel.

sanctify (SANK-tih-fy) To bless or make holy; to set apart for special godly reasons. "May God himself, the God of peace, sanctify you through and through." See *1 Thessalonians 5:23.*

sanctuary (SANK-chu-er-ee) A holy or sacred place; the most sacred place of worship; a building or room for religious worship.

S

Ocean water is full of **SALT**

Sarah (SARE-uh) Abraham's wife who didn't have her first child, Isaac, until she was ninety years old.

Satan (SAY-tun) Another name for the devil; he is the enemy of all humankind. "Satan comes and takes away the word that was sown in them." See *Mark 4:15.*

satisfy (SA-tis-fy) To make content or please; to convince and assure. "He will satisfy your needs in a sun-scorched land . . ." See *Isaiah 58:11.*

Saul (SAWL) He treated Christians very badly, but after a blinding encounter with God, he became a strong preacher of the gospel, and was called Paul.

save (SAYV) To rescue; to put aside or keep. Bob saves all his pennies in a big, pink piggy bank.

Savior (SAVE-yer) A redeemer. This is another name for Jesus who sacrificed his life to be our savior from death and sin. "And we have seen and testify that the Father has sent his Son to be the Savior of the world." See *1 John 4:14.*

Junior saw something **SCARY.**

scary (SKAIR-ee) Frightening or terrifying. Junior Asparagus was frightened by the scary shadows on his wall.

scatter (SKAT-ur) To cause things to separate or spread

out. "[There is] a time to scatter stones and a time to gather them, a time to embrace and a time to refrain..." See *Ecclesiastes 3:5*.

sceptor (SEP-tur) A rod held by royal people as a symbol of power.

schedule (SKEJ-ul) A list of events or tasks to be done in a certain time frame.

scheme (SKEEM) To plan or plot; a system of conspiracy. Poor Thomas had no idea that King George planned a scheme to steal his treasured ducky in "King George and the Ducky."

Scooter (SKOOT-er) A fiesty Veggie carrot with a Scottish accent.

scribe (SKRYB) Someone who copies important writings and numbers. The Scriptures were written by scribes.

Scripture (SKRIP-chur) The inspired words of God found in the Bible. "All Scripture is God-breathed..." See *2 Timothy 3:16*.

scroll (SKROLE) A long piece of paper with writing on it. The books of the Bible were written on scrolls.

SCOOTER

S

SCUBA Stuff-Mart salesmen

scuba (SKOO-buh) A tank of air strapped to your back that allows you to breathe through a hose and mouthpiece while you swim underwater observing things. The Stuff-Mart salesmen dressed in scuba gear to sell it to Madame Blueberry.

Sea of Galilee This body of water is 12 1/2 miles long, and between 80 to 160 feet deep. Its surface is 682 feet below sea level. It is 27 miles east of the Mediterranean, and about 60 miles northeast of Jerusalem. You can read about Jesus walking on the water in the Sea of Galilee in *Matthew 14:22–33*.

search (SURCH) To look for something; to hunt; to investigate. "Search me, O God, and know my heart . . ." See *Psalm 139:23*. Esther searched for wisdom and answers so she would know how to talk to the king.

secret (SEE-kret) Something hidden or kept from knowledge or view. Dr. Jiggle had a secret. He was also Mr. Sly, the fabulous disco dancer.

seek (SEEK) To look for something. "Ask and it will be given to you; seek and you will find . . ." See *Matthew 7:7*.

Self-control (self-kun-TROLE) Not doing things you know to be wrong or bad for you.

selfish (SELF-ish) Wanting

something just for yourself; to be self-centered.

Sermon on the Mount (SUR-mun on the MOWNT) Jesus taught the crowds how to find inner joy in how they act as he spoke on a hill in Galilee. See *Matthew 5–7.*

SEYMOUR SCHWENK

serpent (SER-pent) A snake-like creature.

servant (SER-vant) Someone who works on the behalf of others; someone who waits on someone else's needs. See *John 12:26.*

serve (serv) to do something for the benefit of someone else; to work or assist others.

Seth (SETH) Adam and Eve's third son, born after Abel; died.

Seymour Schwenk (SEE-mor shwenk) A Veggie character who is an inventor in "An Easter Carol."

Shack (SHAK) A Veggie character who works with his brothers, Rack and Benny, at the Chocolate Factory.

Shadrack (SHAD-rak) One of the three friends of Daniel who was thrown into a fiery furnace.

S

share (SHAIR) To let someone use your things; to give some of what you have. "He called you to this through our gospel, that you might share in the glory of our Lord Jesus Christ." See *2 Thessalonians 2:14.* Lyle, the kindly Viking, happily shares his potholders with those in need.

128 sheep · Sidon

sheep (SHEEP) A fluffy barnyard animal often raised for their wool, skin, or meat.

shekel (SHEK-el) An ancient unit of weight or value like money.

Shem (SHEM) Noah's oldest son.

shepherd (SHEP-erd) Someone who takes care of sheep. See *Psalm 23* or *John 10:1–30* to learn more about how Jesus is our Shepherd.

SHERIFF BOB

Sheriff Bob (SHAIR-if BOB) A Veggie character played by Bob the Tomato who upholds the law in "The Ballad of Little Joe."

shield (SHEELD) A piece of armor carried to protect the body.

ship (SHIP) A very large boat or vessel; to send or transport.

shop (SHOP) A store or supermarket; to buy things. Madame Blueberry wanted to shop 'til she dropped at the Stuff-Mart.

shortcoming (SHORT-kuh-ming) A fault.

show (SHOH) To demonstrate; to prove; to allow someone else to see something. "Show me your ways, O LORD, teach me your paths . . ." See *Psalm 25:4*.

sibling (SIB-ling) A sister or brother.

Sidon (SY-dun) A port stop on Paul's journey as a prisoner to Rome.

SILLY SONGS with Larry

Silas (SYE-lus) A companion of Paul who taught in a Jerusalem church. He went to prison with Paul.

silly (SIL-ee) Something goofy that makes you giggle. When Larry wears an oven mitt on his head, he is acting very silly.

Silly Songs (SIL-ee-SONGS) Veggie tunes that tickle your funny bone.

silver (SIL-vur) A shiny gray metal.

Simeon (SIM-ee-un) The second son of Jacob and Leah. The Veggie brother Joseph kept until the others returned with their father.

sight (SITE) The ability to see; to view to sight something; to notice. "We live by faith, not by sight." See *2 Corinthians 5:7*.

sign (SINE) Letters, words, or symbols put together for people to see; a signal.

Simon (SYE-mun) One of Jesus' disciples; a fisherman also known as Simon Peter.

sin (SIN) To break one of God's laws. "If we claim to be without sin, we deceive ourselves and the truth is not in us." See *1 John 1:8*.

S

sinner (SIN-ur) Someone that sins.

skillful (SKIL-ful) Someone who is an expert at something; someone competent and practiced.

SKIPPER
Bob

skipper (SKIP-ur) Someone in charge of a boat crew. As the skipper of the shipwrecked boat, Bob the Tomato had to find a way to help everyone get off the island.

slave (SLAYV) Someone forced to work for someone else without getting paid. "Whoever wants to be first must be your slave . . ." See *Matthew 20:27.*

slavery (SLAYV-ur-ee) The practice of forcing one person to work for another as if they were owned.

sleepy (SLEEP-ee) Tired and in need of sleep. Junior Asparagus is sleepy at bedtime when he sings "My Day" in the "Wonderful World of Autotainment."

sling (SLING) A device used to throw stones.

SLUSHEE

slushee (SLUSH-ee) A frozen fruit drink made of crushed ice and flavoring. Larry loves slushees; the French Peas like to throw them.

small (SMAL) Little in size.

snake (SNAYK) A slithering reptile with no legs. "Which

of you, if his son asks . . . for a fish, will give him a snake?" See *Matthew 7:9–10*.

Snooberry Jell-O® (SNOO-bair-ee JEL-oh) A product found in Snoodleburg that is squirted from thimbuttle plants.

SNOODLE

Snoodle (SNOO-dul) A special Veggie character made by a loving Creator who learns that God made him special.

soar (SORE) To fly high; to ascend. "But those who hope in the LORD . . . will soar on wings like eagles . . ." See *Isaiah 40:31*. After Snoodle Doo met with his Creator, he was able to soar high with his wings.

Sodom (SAH-dum) A city destroyed by sin.

soldier (SOHL-jur) Someone who belongs to an army; a fighter or warrior.

solemn (SOL-um) Very serious; somber; sincere.

Solomon (SOL-uh-mun) King David's son who became king himself; he was very wise and built the temple in Jerusalem.

Larry likes wearing his **SOMBRERO**.

sombrero (som-BRER-oh) A spanish-style hat worn to keep the sun off of the face. Larry wears a sombrero in the "Dance of the Cucumber Silly Song."

S

son (SUN) The male child of a mother and father.

Son of David (SUN of DAY-vid) The family line of King David that Jesus was described as coming from.

Son of God (SUN of GOD) Jesus described as coming from God.

Son of Man (SUN of MAN) Jesus described as coming from God, but also as a human man. "At that time men will see the Son of Man coming in clouds with great power and glory." See *Mark 13:26.*

Song of Songs (SONG of SONGS) The twenty-second book of the Old Testament; focuses on the gift of love that God has given to us; filled with love poems.

sorrow (SAW-roh) Great sadness. "How long must I wrestle with my thoughts and every day have sorrow in my heart?" See *Psalm 13:2.*

sorry (SOR-ee) To feel bad about something that has happened because of involvement in it. "Yet now I am happy, not because you were made sorry, but because your sorrow led you to repentance." See *2 Corinthians 7:9.* Bob was sorry he yelled at Larry for trying to surf in the bathtub.

soul (SOLE) The inner spirit of someone; the heart and very core and character of a person.

source (Sours) The beginning; the point where something starts or comes into being.

sovereign (SOV-rin) Having supreme or absolute power; a ruler.

sower (SOH-er) Someone who plants seeds so that they would grow. See *Matthew 13:18–23* to learn about the parable of the sower.

special (SPEH-shul) Unique, individual; extraordinary and exceptional.

spies (SPYZ) People who secretly gather information; people who discover information undercover. In "Daniel and the Lions' Den," the king's spies watch Daniel as he prays.

Spirit (SPIH-rit) The inner part of someone given by God as a gift when they accept Jesus into his or her heart. A strength, soul, and life-source.

spiritual gifts (SPIH-ri-chul GIFTS) The special abilities and skills we have been given by God to do his work in the world. See *1 Corinthians 12:4–11* to learn what some of the spiritual gifts are.

spurs (SPURS) Sharp, pointy stars on the heel of a boot used to spike the ground as someone walks.

squander (SKWAN-der) To spend foolishly or wastefully. Bob told Larry not to squander his money on food for his dust bunnies, but Larry usually didn't listen.

squash (SKWASH) To flatten. A vegetable in the gourd family.

staff (STAF) A long stick used to help someone walk; often carried by shepherds or great servants of God like Moses.

STAINED GLASS

stained glass (STAYND GLAS) Colored glass put together in a way to create art. The stained-glass windows at St. Bart's church tell the story of Jesus' life in "An Easter Carol."

S

stand (STAND) To act on a strong opinion; to remain true to something or someone; to support oneself on the feet. Rack, Shack, and Benny decided to stand up for what they believe in at Mr. Nezzer's chocolate factory. From the video "Rack, Shack, and Benny."

starve (STARV) To be without enough food.

steal (STEEL) To take something without permission.

Stephen (STEE-ven) A great teacher and person of much faith. He followed Jesus and was stoned to death because of it.

stoned (STOHND) The result of having stones thrown at someone.

storehouse (STOR-haus) A building for storing goods; a large supply; a repository.

storm (STORM) An outburst of bad weather; an explosion or eruption of anger. "Without warning, a furious storm came up on the lake, so that the waves swept over the boat." See *Matthew 8:24.*

David showed great **STRENGTH.**

story (STOR-ee) A tale; something told that is sometimes real, sometimes make-believe.

stranger (STRAIN-jur) Someone whom you do not know. "I was a stranger and you invited me in . . ." See *Matthew 25:35.*

strength (STRENGTH) Power or force, either physical or emotional; energy; intensity. "Love the Lord your God with all your heart and with all your soul and with all your mind and with all your strength." See *Mark 12:30.* Although the Giant Pickle showed great strength, he was no match for Dave in "Dave and the Giant Pickle."

struggle (STRU-gul) To wrestle with something; to resist or fight back; to exert great effort in something. "For our struggle is not against flesh and blood, but against the rulers, against the authorities, against the powers of this dark world . . ." See *Ephesians 6:12.*

stuck (STUK) Unable to move.

Stuff-Mart (STUF-mart) The store where Madame Blueberry buys all her stuff. Best known for its wide selection of big screen televisions, grandfather clocks, snorkels, and electric lawn equipment.

stumble (STUM-bul) To make a mistake; to hesitate; to trip your feet when walking or running.

success (SUK-ses) To accomplish or complete something in a good way.

suffer (SUF-ur) To go through great pain or upset; to endure or put up with. "Now for a little while you may have had to suffer grief in all kinds of trials." See *1 Peter 1:6.*

Sumo (SOO-moh) A Japanese form of wrestling.

survive (sur-VIVE) To remain alive; to exist despite challenges.

SVEN

Sven (SVEN) A Veggie Viking character played by Larry the Cucumber. Sven lost the right horn from his helmet during a horrible finger paint battle at Viking summer camp.

swaddling cloths (SWAD-ling CLOTHS) Pieces of material babies are wrapped in when they are very small.

sword (SORD) A large blade used as a weapon. "Take the helmet of salvation and the sword of the Spirit, which is the word of God." See *Ephesians 6:17.*

Sychar (SYE-car) A town in Samaria that Jesus visited and met the woman at the well.

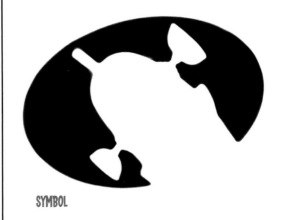

SYMBOL

symbol (SIM-bul) A sign; a representation of something else; an image. "And it will be like a sign on your hand and a symbol on your forehead that the LORD brought us out of Egypt with his mighty hand." See *Exodus 13:16.*

sympathy (SIM-puh-thee) To have understanding of what someone else is going through; to show compassion.

synagogue (SIH-nuh-gog) A Jewish place of worship and schooling.

Syria (SIH-ree-uh) An area north of Galilee that Paul visited on his journeys.

tabernacle (TAB-ur-nak-ul) A tent used by the Israelites as a place of worship, teaching, and meeting.

talent (TAL-ent) A skill; an ability to do something; a gift from God; a monetary unit from Jesus' time. Lyle, the kindly Viking, had the talent for making potholders.

Tarshish (TAR-shish) A city west of the Mediterranean Sea that Jonah headed for instead of Nineveh.

Tarsus (TAR-sus) A city in Cilicia; Saul's hometown.

TAX COLLECTOR

task (TASK) A job; a chore. Rack, Shack, and Benny's task was to make chocolate bunnies.

tax collector (TAX cuh-LEC-tur) A Jew hired to collect taxes for the Romans. Zaccheus was a tax collector.

teach (TEECH) To educate someone; to instruct or train; to explain something. "Teacher, we know that you speak and teach what is right, and that you do not show partiality but teach the way of God in accordance with the truth." See *Luke 20:21*.

S
T

teachings (TEECH-ings) The specific instructions of someone. "So then, brothers, stand firm and hold to the teachings we passed on to you, whether by word of mouth or by letter." See *2 Thessalonians 2:15*. The teachings of Rack, Shack, and Benny's parents helped them to remember not to eat too much chocolate.

teamwork (TEEM-wurk) To get a job done together with others; cooperating with other people to do something. Josh enjoyed the teamwork of his fellow marchers in bringing down the wall in Jericho.

tell (TEL) To talk to about something. "Go home to your family and tell them how much the Lord has done for you, and how he has had mercy on you." See *Mark 5:19*. Bob the Tomato likes to tell the story of "A Snoodle's Tale."

temper (TEM-pur) The way anger shows itself; an attitude that shows annoyance. Junior Asparagus showed his temper to the Grapes of Wrath when they laughed at him.

temple (TEM-pul) A place of worship.

Little Joe resisted the **TEMPTATION.**

temptation (temp-TAY-shun) Something that is luring or attractive to someone. "Watch and pray so that you will not fall into temptation." See *Matthew 26:41*. Little Joe resisted the temptation to take the bag of money from Miss Kitty.

Ten Commandments (TEN cuh-MAND-ments) The ten

rules that God gave to Moses on Mt. Sinai.

test (TEST) An exam taken to see if you know certain information; a trial to make an assessment or conclusion.

testament (TES-tuh-ment) A promise between God and man; evidence of an agreement. The Bible has two major parts, the Old Testament and the New Testament.

testify (TES-ti-fy) To give witness to what you believe. "I tell you the truth, we speak of what we know, and we testify to what we have seen . . ." See *John 3:11.*

testimony (TES-ti-moh-ne) Firsthand evidence; a public declaration of one's faith experience.

Thaddaeus (THAD-ee-us) One of Jesus' twelve apostles.

thank (THANK) To express that you are grateful. Larry called Bob to thank him for taking over the show when he wasn't there.

thankfulness (THANK-full-ness) Full of gladness and appreciation.

THANKSGIVING is the holiday to think about what you're thankful for.

thanksgiving (thanks-GIV-ing) Giving thanks; feeling grateful for; a blessing. "I will praise God's name in song and glorify him with thanksgiving." See *Psalm 69:30.*

THE PEACH

The Peach (the PEECH) A Veggie character with the best hairdo. Larry gave The Peach his special hairbrush.

The Pirates Who Don't Do Anything A fun-loving group of pirates who enjoy taking it easy and not working. What do they do? They don't do anything!

1 Thessalonians (FURST thes-uh-LOH-nee-uns) The eighth book of letters in the New Testament, written by Paul to tell the people that Jesus was coming back and to thank them for their faith.

2 Thessalonians (SEK-und thes-uh-LOH-nee-uns) The ninth book of letters in the New Testament, written by Paul to clarify questions people had in his first group of letters to them.

Thessalonica (thes-uh-luh-NY-kuh) Capital of Macedonia, which is now in northern Greece; named after the sister of Alexander the Great. Paul wrote 1 and 2 Thessalonians to the Christians in this city.

thief (THEEF) Someone who takes things without asking; a robber or crook. "The day of the Lord will come like a thief in the night." See *1 Thessalonians 5:2*. The Milk Money Bandit is a thief who takes milk money. Larryboy to the rescue!

thimbuttle plants (THIM-buh-tul PLANTS) A Veggie plant that grows in Snoodle-burg and squirts Snooberry Jell-O®.

and they are usually hungry for cheese curls.

Thomas (TOM-us) One of Jesus' twelve disciples who had great love for Jesus. He is, however, also known as "doubting Thomas" because he doubted Jesus had risen from the dead.

threat (THRET) A warning that something bad may happen. Awful Alvin made a threat to Larryboy that he would rule Bumblyburg with his over-easy eggray.

throne (THROHN) A fancy chair where royalty sits.

Tigris (TYE-gris) A river that bordered Eden found in the mountains of Turkey.

time (TYM) An occasion; a phase or cycle of seconds, minutes, hours, days, or a life; an era. "There is a time for everything, and a season for every activity under heaven . . ." See *Ecclesiastes 3:1.*

Larry's **THINKING.**

think (THINGK) The process of considering things with your mind; to believe; to reason. Larry thinks about all sorts of things, like rockets, dust bunnies, and how much God loves him!

thirst (THIRST) A need to drink. The Pirates Who Don't Do Anything thirst for rootbeer,

T

Timothy (TIM-uh-thee) A close friend of Paul who traveled with him a great deal.

1 Timothy (FURST TIM-uh-thee) The tenth book of letters in the New Testament, written by Paul to Timothy to guide him as a leader and give instruction for how the church should be run.

2 Timothy (SEK-und TIM-uh-thee) The eleventh book of letters in the New Testament, written by Paul to Timothy encouraging Timothy's ministry after Paul has died.

The pirates are **TIRED.**

tired (TY-erd) The feeling of being sleepy, worn out, or weary. The Pirates Who Don't Do Anything are too tired to do anything. (Zip, zilch, nada!)

tithe (TYTH) To give a portion of one's earnings back to God.

Titus (TYE-tus) The twelfth book of letters in the New Testament, written by Paul to Titus to encourage him as he works with the church in Crete.

together (too-GEH-thur) With others. "For where two or three come together in my name, there am I with them." See *Matthew 18:20*. Bob and Larry are frequently seen together on the kitchen counter.

TOM

Tom (TOM) A grape Veggie character; brother to Rosie.

T

Bob is a **TOMATO**.

tomato (tuh-MAY-toh) A round, usually red, juicy vegetable. Kids' favorite tomato is Bob the Tomato.

tomb (TOOM) A place where dead people are buried; in Bible times, this was usually a place in the side of a mountain or in a cave, both of which were enclosed in some way afterward.

Tower of Babel (TOW-ur of BAB-ul) A structure that was being built in the city of Babel, with each higher level smaller than the one before it. The people believed they could build it high enough to reach heaven. See the explanation in *Genesis 11:1–9*.

town (TOUN) An area where people live, usually larger than a village and smaller than a city. Two of the towns in VeggieTales are Flibber-o-loo and Jibberty-lot.

trade (TRAYD) A skill someone is trained at; to exchange something for something else.

tradition (truh-DIH-shun) A custom, activity, or belief that is passed along from generation to generation. It was the tradition in Flibber-o-loo to wear shoes on your head, whereas, in Jibberty-lot, they wore pots.

traitor (TRATE-er) Someone who betrays anothers trust or is false to an obligation or duty. Judas was a traitor to Jesus. See *Matthew 26:25*.

T

Bob likes to **TRAVEL**.

Transfiguration (trans-FIG-yur-ay-shun) A special event in which the disciples Peter, James, and John were spoken to by God and realized that things had changed. God told them that Jesus was his Son, and that they should obey only him from then on. You can read about it in *Matthew 17:1–9.*

transgression (trans-GREH-shun) To sin; to break a law. Bob is not always so quick to forgive Larry for his silly transgressions.

transport (trans-PORT) To move things from one place to another. Chocolate bunnies are transported on an assembly line in "Rack, Shack, and Benny."

travel (TRA-vul) To go somewhere; to take a journey. You probably don't want to travel to the Island of Perpetual Tickling.

treasure (TREH-zhur) Things of great value; riches or jewels kept and sometimes hidden in a box. "Do not store up for yourselves treasures on earth . . ." See *Matthew 6:19.*

tree house (TREE-hous) A house in a tree; Madame Blueberry lives in one.

tree of knowledge A special tree that God created in the Garden of Eden that produced fruit that Adam and Eve were not to eat. See *Genesis 2:9* to read about how God created the tree of knowledge.

tree of life A special tree in the Garden of Eden. See *Genesis 3:22.* By eating the fruit from this tree a person was kept from dying.

tremble (trem-bul) To shake uncontrollably; to be very afraid.

trespass (TRES-pas) To do something that is wrong; to sin.

trial (TRY-ul) A test; a hardship; a formal court hearing. Read about facing trials in *James 1:12.*

tribe (TRYB) A group of similar people; descendants of someone. Israel had twelve tribes that were the descendants of Jacob.

trip (TRIP) A journey somewhere; to stumble or fall. The Pirates Who Don't Do Anything dream of taking a trip to Boston in the fall.

triumph (TRY-umf) To achieve victory; to succeed.

triumphal entry (tri-UM-ful en-TREE) Jesus' entry into Jerusalem just before his death. People gathered and cheered him as their king, spread their coats on the ground, and waved palm branches.

Troas (TRO-as) A city in northwest Asia; this was one of the stops in Paul's travels.

trouble (TRUH-bul) A problem or worry; a difficult situation; a mess. To bother or worry about. "In this world you will have trouble. But take heart! I have overcome the world." See *John 16:33.*

Madame Blueberry lives in a **TREE HOUSE.**

Larry plays the **TUBA**.

trumpet (TRUM-pet) A horn instrument that plays a bright sound.

trust (TRUST) To have faith and belief in; to have confidence in someone or some-thing. "Trust in the LORD with all your heart and lean not on your own under-standing . . ." See *Proverbs 3:5.*

trustworthy (TRUST-wur-thee) To be dependable, responsible, and honest.

truth (TROOTH) A fact of honesty. "In reply Jesus declared, 'I tell you the truth, no one can see the kingdom of God unless he is born again.'" See *John 3:3.*

tuba (TOO-bah) A large, winding horn instrument that plays a deep sound. Larry is an excellent tuba player.

tunic (TOO-nik) A piece of clothing that hangs down to the knees and was worn in ancient Greece and Rome; a dress for men.

Twippo (TWIH-poh) A beloved Veggie singer/per-former played by Archibald Asparagus in "Jonah, a VeggieTales Movie."

TWIPPO

understand (un-der-STAND) To realize something; to know what is happening; to recognize or be aware of. *Esther understands that she may become a queen for a purpose.*

unfailing (un-FAY-ling) Constant, not likely to change. God's love for us is unfailing. See *Psalm 13:5.*

ungrateful (un-GRAYT-ful) Not thankful; not showing any appreciation for something.

unlawful (un-LAW-ful) Against the law.

unleavened bread (un-LEV-und BRED) A thick, flat cracker made without yeast.

T
U

unity (YOO-nih-tee) Standing together; having harmony; agreement. "And over all these virtues put on love, which binds them all together in perfect unity." See *Colossians 3:14.*

unchanging (un-CHANJ-ing) Not altering or to making different.

unclean (un-KLEEN) Not pleasing to God; not clean.

unrighteous (un-RY-chus) Doing things that are not right; to do wrong.

unsuitable (un-SOOT-uh-bul) Not able to use.

unveil (un-VALE) To show something for the first time. Edmund Gilbert is going to unveil the Star of Christmas at the Christmas Eve pageant.

unworthy (un-WUR-thee) Lacking in excellence or worth; not deserving.

uphold (up-HOLD) To support; to defend.

upper room (UP-ur ROOM) A place where Jesus and his disciples shared the Last Supper.

upset (UP-set) Troubled; disturbed; saddened; stirred up. Bob's tummy was upset when he ate too many sardines.

Ur (YOOR) A city where Abraham lived.

urge (URJ) To encourage; to plead; to feel the need to. "I urge you, brothers, by our Lord Jesus Christ and by the love of the Spirit, to join me in my struggle by praying to God for me" See *Romans 15:30.* Bob urged Madame Blueberry to resist the urge to splurge at the Stuff-Mart.

Uriah (yoo-RYE-uh) A soldier in King David's army, he was married to Bathsheba and killed in battle.

U.S.S. APPLEPIES

U.S.S. Applepies (U.S.S. AP-ul-pyz) A spaceship in the video, "God Wants Me to Forgive Them?"

Uzzah (UH-zuh) A man who died when he touched the

ark of the covenant that God had forbidden to touch.

Uzziah(uh-ZYE-uh) The king of Judah who became very proud and was punished by God.

valley (VAL-ee) The land between two mountains or hills. *A valley ran between the towns of Flibber-o-loo and Jibberty-lot.*

Valley of Hebron (VAL-ee of HEE-brun) A large area between the mountains that held Canaan and Shechem.

vanish (VAN-ish) To pass from sight or existence.

Vashti (VASH-tee) King Xerxes' first wife who was removed, allowing Esther to eventually become queen.

vast (VAST) Very large; huge; great. "How precious to me are your thoughts, O God! How vast is the sum of them!" See *Psalm 139:17.*

vegetables (VEJ-tuh-buls) Food that comes from plants. Real vegetables are not Veggies. Veggies are not real vegetables.

Veggies (VEH-jees) A nickname for any of the VeggieTales characters.

VEGGIES

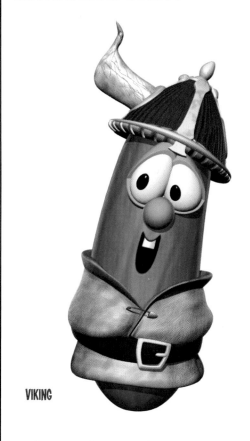

Big Idea's **VEGGIETALES**

VeggieTales (VEH-jee-TAYLS) Big Idea's Veggie-Tales is a family entertainment series designed to help parents teach timeless Christian values like honesty, kindness, and forgiveness in delightfully wacky ways.

veil (VALE) A thin garment worn over one's face.

vengeance (VEN-juns) Punishment given in return for an injury or offense.

verdict (VER-dikt) The decision reached by a jury; judgment; opinion.

verse (VERS) A stanza or line within a larger written structure. The Bible consists of sixty-six books. Each book is divided into chapters compiled of various verses.

victory (VIC-tuh-ree) Triumph; winning or success. "But thanks be to God! He gives us the victory through our Lord Jesus Christ." See *1 Corinthians 15:57.*

VIKING

Viking (VYE-king) A pirate from the country of Norway. In "Lyle the Kindly Viking," Lyle was a very kind and gentle Viking.

village (VIL-ij) A small town in the countryside. The

village of West Manor is the home to the peas that say please and thank you.

vine (VYN) A climbing plant. "I am the vine; you are the branches." See *John 15:5.*

vineyard (VIN-yard) A field of grapevines.

vision (VIH-zhun) Something that is like a dream with a point; a given foresight of what is to come or what may be. Bob had a vision that Larry would make people laugh.

visitor (VIZ-uh-tur) A guest.

voice (VOYS) The sound made when someone speaks; the influence or controlling power behind an idea. "We all fell to the ground, and I heard a voice saying to me in Aramaic, 'Saul, Saul, why do you persecute me?'" See *Acts 26:14.* The Snoodle heard his Creator's voice, and he was reassured that he was special and loved.

vow (VOU) A promise.

voyage (VOY-ij) A journey.

Larry is **WACKY.**

wacky (WAK-ee) A fun, silly, madcap humor or expression, often found in VeggieTales.

wages (WAY-ges) Payment or earnings for something done.

wailing (WAYL-ing) Crying; moaning; weeping.

WALLY P. NEZZER

W

Wally P. Nezzer (WAHL-ee PEE NEZ-er) Owner of the chocolate factory; believes chocolate bunnies are the best thing out there.

wander (WAN-dur) To roam about.

war (WOR) A time of armed, hostile conflict between states, nations, or groups; a struggle between opposing forces.

warn (WORN) To caution; to give notice before something bad happens. "And we urge you, brothers, warn those who are idle, encourage the timid, help the weak, be patient with everyone." See *1 Thessalonians 5:14*.

warrior (WOR-ee-ur) Someone who fights on behalf of a cause; a soldier.

water buffalo (WAH-tur BUF-uh-loh) A mammal that everybody loves. Everybody's got a water buffalo; some are fast and some are slow! Oh, where we get them I don't know, but everybody's got a water buffalo!

way (WAY) A path to get from one place to another; a direction; a method or means. "Jesus answered, 'I am the way and the truth and the life.'" See *John 14:6.*

weak (WEEK) Not strong; tired.

weapon (WEH-pun) A tool used to hurt people.

wedding (WED-ing) The ceremony where a man and woman become huband and wife. Esther and King Xerxes held a wedding in which Esther was then made queen.

weep (WEEP) To cry.

weigh (WAY) To measure how heavy something is.

well (WEL) A deep hole in the ground in which water or something is gathered using a rope, bucket, and crank; being healthy; feeling good.

wept (WEPT) Cried hard. "Jesus wept." See *John 11:35.*

whale (WAYL) The Largest mammal to live in the ocean. Jonah was swallowed by a great whale that eventually spit him back out again.

wheat (WHEET) A grain used to make many foods.

whine (WYN) To complain; to whimper. Larry often whines when Bob won't let him put marshmallows in the spaghetti sauce.

WEEP

W

whisper (WHIS-pur) To use a very quiet voice; to speak softly. "He stilled the storm to a whisper; the waves of the sea were hushed." See *Psalm 107:29.*

wholehearted (hole-HAR-ted) Enthusiastic, determined, and devoted.

wicked (WIK-ed) Very evil; bad; wrong.

widow (WID-oh) A woman whose husband has died.

wilderness (WIL-der-nes) An area of nature unchanged by humans.

will (WILL) What someone wants to happen; determination; a desire. "For I have come down from heaven not to do my will but to do the will of him who sent me." See *John 6:38.*

wisdom (WIZ-dum) To have great knowledge and understanding. "But the wisdom that comes from heaven is first of all pure; then peace-loving . . ." See *James 3:17.*

wise (WYZ) Very knowledgeable and full of wisdom. Because Pa Grape is wise, he helps train the Itallian Scallion in "Sumo of the Opera."

wise men (WYZ men) Men with great knowledge and understanding who studied the stars. There were wise men who followed the star that led to Jesus when he was born.

WISHING you learn a lot.

wishing (WISH-ing) To hope for something. Bob and

Larry are wishing that you learn a lot from reading the Veggie Bible Dictionary!

witness (WIT-nes) A person who has seen or heard something. "You will be my witnesses in Jerusalem, and in all Judea and Samaria, and to the ends of the earth." See *Acts 1:8.*

woe (WO) Great suffering from loss, misfortune, or trouble; sorrow.

womb (WOOM) The place inside a woman where a baby grows.

wonder (WON-der) Something extraordinary or surprising; marvel; a feeling caused by something extraordinary.

wonderful (WON-der-ful) Full of wonder; magnificent; great. "And he will be called Wonderful Counselor, Mighty God . . ." See *Isaiah 9:6* to read about the prophesy of God's Son.

Word (WURD) God's breathed message to us through the Bible; a combination of letters that represent something; the gospel. "So is my word that goes out from my mouth: It will not return to me empty . . ." See *Isaiah 55:11.*

work (WURK) To labor or exert effort to get a job done; employment. Lyle works hard to make his potholders.

Construction **WORKER**

W

worker (WURK-er) Someone who does work.

world (WURLD) The planet earth that God created. "He's got the whole world in his hands."

worship (WUR-ship) To praise. "Worship him who made the heavens, the earth, the sea and the springs of water." See *Revelation 14:7*. Jonah worshiped God in the belly of the whale in the movie "Jonah, a VeggieTales Movie."

worthless (WURTH-les) Not valuable.

worthy (WUR-thee) Having worth or value.

wrath (RATH) Extreme anger or rage.

wrestle (RES-el) To struggle with and try to throw down an opponent; to struggle for control. The Italian Scallion had to wrestle Apollo Gourd. in "The Sumo of the Opera."

W
X

wrong (RAWNG) Mistaken or incorrect; false. Junior admitted that he was wrong for not admitting that he broke his dad's plate.

XERXES

Xerxes (ZERK-seez) The King that Esther married.

Yahweh (YAH-weh) Another name for God.

yeast (YEEST) An ingredient used in baking.

yodel (YOH-dul) A musical form of the voice. In the Silly Song, "Yodeling Veterinarian of the Alps," Larry plays an animal doctor who likes to yodel.

This veterinarian likes to **YODEL**.

yoke (YOHK) A wooden frame worn by oxen that keeps them close together while they work. "For my yoke is easy and my burden is light." See *Matthew 11:30.*

youth (YOOTH) The time of life when one is young; especially the period between childhood and adulthood. In *Psalm 119:9,* the Bible says that youth can live a pure life by obeying God's Word.

yummy (YUM-ee) Very pleasing and delicious, especially to the taste. Jimmy and Jerry Gourd thought that all of the food was very yummy. Especially the caramel-covered pizza!

Y
Z

Zaccheus (za-KEE-us) A tax collector who saw the errors of his ways and became a follower of Jesus.

zeal (ZEEL) To have a great enthusiasm or passion for something. "Never be lacking in zeal, but keep your spiritual fervor, serving the Lord." See *Romans 12:11*.

zealots (ZEL-uts) A group of Jewish men who hated the Romans.

Zebedee (ZEH-beh-dee) The father of the disciples James and John.

Zebulun (ZEB-yuh-lun) Leah and Jacob's sixth son.

Zechariah (zech-uh-RYE-uh) The thirty-eighth book of the Old Testament; this prophet taught people about God and motivated the rebuilding of the temple.

Zee (ZEE) The expression used by the French Peas in place of the word "the" due to their French accents. "We are zee French Peas, and we like zee opera!" says the French Peas.

Zephaniah (zef-uh-NY-uh) The thirty-sixth book of the Old Testament; named after the prophet who warned the people of Judah about God's judgment.

Ziba (ZY-buh) Saul's servant put in charge of his crippled son.

Zilpah (ZIL-puh) Maidservant of Jacob's wife Leah.

Zion (ZY-un) Another name for the City of David, Jerusalem.

Zipporah (zih-POR-uh) The wife of Moses.

zither (ZI-ther) In biblical times, an instrument with thirty to forty tuned strings that are plucked with the fingers or with a pick.

zzzzzzz The sound Bob and Larry are making. They just fell asleep, but they want you to remember God made you special, and he loves you very much!